Liberty & Prosperity

Liberal economics for achieving universal prosperity

Gopi Krishna Suvanam

Series in Economics

 VERNON PRESS

www.vernonpress.com

In the Americas:	*In the rest of the world:*
Vernon Press	Vernon Press
1000 N West Street, Suite 1200	C/Sancti Espiritu 17,
Wilmington, Delaware, 19801	Malaga, 29006
United States	Spain

Series in Economics

Library of Congress Control Number: 2021931317

ISBN: 978-1-64889-198-4

Cover design by Vernon Press. Cover image by ejaugsburg from Pixabay.

Table of contents

List of figures

List of tables

Preface

As a result of the financial crisis of 2008 and various governments' responses to that, there is a disillusionment amongst different segments of the society concerning the role of governments and central banks. The bailout of banks by governments is seen as a regressive move and central banks are no longer seen as know-all, wise entities. There have been several counter-movements because of this disillusionment including the tea party movement, occupy wall street movement. Although it is clear that what governments and central banks are doing right now is not perfect, people are not clear about the alternative framework that could work. This book is an attempt to illuminate an alternative policy framework using liberal economic policies. It has evolved over the years based on my personal and professional experience looking at economies around the world.

As the book is more of a book on economics and does not intend to be political in nature, recent events and current policies are not discussed in detail, but the principles elaborated in the book have direct applicability in the current world. The ideas discussed are intended for countries in different stages of development and are not restricted to either developed countries or emerging economies. The main aim of the book is to examine what we as a society can do to achieve universal prosperity. The recurrent topic in the book is that liberty and prosperity are intertwined as without prosperity man cannot have true liberty and on the other hand, the best way to achieve universal prosperity is through providing liberty to all.

The book does not necessarily bring out new research but identifies the right measures from existing liberal theories that could work in the long term. Thus the book can be said to be in continuation in the tradition of classical liberalism. Having said that there will be a few contrarian ideas that will be discussed especially on taxation and money. There are a few books that aim to prescribe economic solutions to the problems in the post-2008 world. Some of those books take the approach of the free market, liberal economic policies that the current book takes. Most of the ideas presented in those books are innovative but many of them may not be practicable immediately. I do not intend to bring out radical, futuristic ideas, but stick to well thought out solutions from classical liberal economic frameworks. There are some other popular books in economics recently published, that do not look at economics from a (classical) liberal lens. Many of them have an interventionist approach and also give micro-level recommendations rather than discussing macro-ideas. On the other hand, classical books, published several decades ago, like Henry George's *"Progress and Poverty"* and F. A. Hayek's *"Constitution of Liberty"* contain liberal, macro ideas. I will revisit a lot of those ideas in the current context.

One set of audience for the book will be people who understand the economy and business a little bit but do not have an in-depth understanding of economics. Another set of audience will be students who want to get an overview of classical macroeconomic principles. A few chapters contain contrarian/novel ideas, which will be of interest to professional economists as well. These chapters can initiate new debates, which can guide economic thought and policy frameworks. The language of the book is kept simple with minimal jargon so that the reader can walk through the ideas without much background knowledge. The book slowly builds on various ideas and some ideas are recurrent to drive them home. There are embedded references to economists, authors, and other books so that readers can dig deeper into specific topics. Hopefully, the book can create awareness about classical liberal economics to battle current day problems.

Part 1: Introduction

Chapter 1

On the conspicuous absence
of universal prosperity

It aches me to see, even after decades of economic and industrial growth, a significant portion of the human population still living in absolute or relative poverty when the premise of growth is that it brings prosperity to all. This is in spite of using scientific methods to manage economies starting with Adam Smith in the eighteenth century. I'm not contesting the fact that there have been significant improvements in human life and there are many things to look forward to, including a drop in absolute poverty levels, improvement in infant mortality rates, and the rise in life expectancy. Nevertheless, the pursuit of economists should not stop until every human being has enough prosperity to fulfill all of her (reasonable) aspirations and not just the basic need for food and protection. Of course, it can be said that the aspirations will keep increasing, but looking at the current state of affairs, humans are still way behind reaching a state where most of them can be said to be able to achieve their reasonable aspirations and lead a happy life by any measure.

When one walks in the streets of slums in Mumbai or visits the favelas of Rio de Janeiro or dwells in the villages of sub-Saharan Africa, the fact that we need to achieve much more becomes quite obvious. That is not the end of it, even New York City and London or the perfectly manicured urban spaces of Dubai and Singapore have residents who are in poverty - some in absolute poverty and a lot in relative poverty. Where billionaires are being made from the trade of oil or diamonds or financial securities, or of late building technology solutions, the poor and also the not so poor struggle to lead a happy life on a daily basis. Where people spend $1,000 or more on a meal, there are people living on less than $1 a day. This is an extreme case of disparity but even on a more moderate level, drastic inequalities are visible everywhere, even if one chooses to ignore them or get used to them.

The cause of this persistent ailment has baffled some economists, but most of them have brushed it aside arguing that with growth there will be prosperity for everyone - eventually. But the time has now come to question if that hypothesis is true. And if that hypothesis is true, why are we not growing fast enough to make prosperity for everyone imminent? It can be fairly argued that past decades of liberal economic policies around the world (after World War II) have shown secular growth and have created enough wealth at an aggregate level. But the question - why are we not growing fast enough for us to be already prosperous - remains, and other related questions arise: even if growth could solve the problem of poverty and create universal prosperity, are there any other policy measures that could be taken to spread the effect of growth to everyone faster? The rest of the book tries to answer these two questions: How do we grow faster? Other than fostering economic growth, what else is needed for quickening the journey to universal prosperity?

The first of the questions is similar to what economists call the problem of efficiency and the second is similar to what they call the problem of equity/distribution. I would use these terms sparingly, as firstly they carry a legacy of left-wing versus right-wing debate, and secondly, they may not fully represent the nuances of universal prosperity the way I have phrased it above. Also both the questions may be intricately related to each other - perhaps without achieving equity we may not get full efficiency and vice versa. Some economists focus solely on efficiency and ignore the problem of equity and some the other way round. This may not serve the purpose of either of the objectives fully. The last century has validated free-market economics and liberal policies for achieving high growth, especially in emerging economies. But this century is seeing the effects of some policy mistakes. Policy mistakes accumulated towards the end of the twentieth century, have led to asset bubbles, wealth disparities, and emanating slowdown in growth. As a result, the world is moving towards a protectionist approach, rather than fixing what is wrong with free-market economics. That seems like a step backward.

A shortcut answer some economists give for the question of lack of prosperity is the rapid growth in population. That would be a lazy approach though, as for several decades the world economy has been growing at a faster rate than its population. Besides, it may seem that having fewer people to share nature's resources would make more available to each one of them, but it can also be argued that having more population, with an abundance of capable workforce, can increase overall production in the economy. "Demographic dividend" is a fancy name given to this. Countries like India have a demographic dividend for some time without reaping many benefits out of it yet, not because of a lack of natural resources or capital but because of a lack of opportunities to deploy the workforce, the resources, and the capital.

Here one could argue that the effects and opportunities offered by free-market economics have not been able to reach the grassroots level. This may not be because of some fundamental flaw in liberal economic theory, but because of certain deficiencies in the real world, which are assumed away by economists, including monopolization of land, frictions in the movement of goods and capital, etc. The approach I'm going to take in this book is not to question already established liberal economic theories, as recommendations from these theories have been proven to spur efficiency across the globe, but to try to come up with a systematic set of steps that could help humanity in achieving prosperity using liberal policies.

Other than from an efficiency angle, the reason I'm strongly advocating liberal economic policies is the moral angle of liberty. Societal restrictions on trade and economic activity, in general, have been recent phenomena. Man has been engaging in these activities freely for millennia before various governments decided to intervene and reduce this liberty. A non-interventionist and liberal government is a step towards reestablishing natural order. So apart from efficiency and equity, moral justice becomes another goal to evaluate various economic policy decisions. Nobel laureate Friedrich A. Hayek brilliantly argued in his book *The Road to Serfdom* that liberty is the only guiding force for governance and any deviation from this concept can lead to misery[1]. He proclaims that any step towards controlling freedom, including the ones to support the weak, will eventually lead to severe restrictions of freedom hurting everyone. Practically though, I believe that some regulation/control is inevitable. For example, hurting others and stealing others' property has to be prohibited and those prohibitions have to be implemented by law. The same can be said about certain economic activities, especially activities that involve other humans, land, and other natural resources. So the question that remains is how much control and intervention is okay? I will try to examine these issues very carefully through the subsequent chapters.

The last few decades have given further meaning to liberty because one can do more things with liberty. One can sell services to a company in California sitting in Bangalore or in the Philippines. One can access the latest news, entertainment from anywhere in the world. One can experiment and build new things with very little cost. One can express views and exchange information instantaneously with a large group of audience. The fact that more can be done with liberty now means that the impact of liberal policies will be much more now than ever.

Starting from Adam Smith to Milton Friedman, there have been several economists arguing for liberal economic policies with free markets. I'm not going to try to reinvent the wheel. I would rather build upon their arguments, critically examining them in the light of economic development over the last two and a half centuries, as some of their ideas have been rejected for non-

---

[1] Hayek, F. A. (1994). *The road to serfdom. 50th anniversary edition with a new introductiom by Milton Friedman.* Chicago: University of Chicago Press.

economic reasons and some of their ideas have not yielded expected results. In the next chapter, I want to establish how prosperity is dependent on economic liberty. Subsequent chapters elaborate upon the details of economic liberty.

Chapter 2

On economic liberty

Very few people will put their hands up and say they oppose liberty, although the actions and subsequent caveats of those who support liberty will immediately show that, in fact, very few people actually support liberty to the fullest extent (maybe including me). "I support liberty, but…" - they would say. There is always a "but" as different people put different caveats to liberty. What comes after "but" is very crucial. Liberty comes in several facets - political, social, and economic; most people only support one of the facets, i.e. their notion of liberty. Our chief concern here is economic liberty although I advocate all forms of liberty. In fact, Friedrich August von Hayek argued, in his book The Road to Serfdom, that any curtailing of economic freedoms would eventually lead to curtailing of all liberties. Socialist governments turning to autocracies in the past have supported his argument. That has been true in most cases in the past, although there have been counterexamples as well, where high state intervention in economics, through democratic socialism, did not lead to a fascist regime. What it has led to is a slow-growing economy with low per capita income.

As most people support only one form of liberty, the meaning of the word "liberal" has also been interpreted quite differently over time and by different people. Currently, it carries the connotation of being socially liberal. I consider myself a liberal but do not want to restrict the meaning to being socially liberal. Some people suggest the right word to use then would be "libertarian" - someone who supports social, political, and economic liberties. Current libertarian thought is not homogenous with several sub-categories within it, so I want to use the term cautiously. Another suggestion is to use the word "classical-liberal" in the sense of liberalism propounded by Adam Smith, John Locke, and other early liberals. The word "classical" is added to distinguish it from the liberal movement of the twentieth century, which had left leanings when it came to economics. I do not want to use this term as it is typically used in a retrospective sense to distinguish earlier liberalism from the twentieth century's social liberalism. Neo-liberalism is a term with a similar meaning; it does not make a good choice for me, as the word "neo" indicates something new, whereas the concepts I'm going to propound have been existent for quite some time. Thus I will stick to the term "liberal" - with the intended meaning of 'supporter of all types of liberties'. Having said that, the goal of this book is to examine liberal economic policies and the impact of them on prosperity, so I will restrain myself from commenting on political and social aspects unless they have an impact on our end objective. When talking about economic freedom, I will use the terms "economic liberal" and "libertarian" synonymously; "libertarian", being a single word, fits better in certain grammatical constructs.

Economic liberty and prosperity are intertwined closely. Economic liberty gives the platform for individuals, corporations, and nations to excel at their performance. This contributes to the wealth of the society and as a result, the prosperity of the individual. This is not just a theoretical concept, although it has been established through rigorous analytical frameworks. More importantly, the link between economic liberty and prosperity has been established through empirical evidence across countries and across time periods. On the analytical front, it has been proven that if all markets operate in perfect competition, where all goods and services are freely traded without any friction (like transaction costs, etc.) an economy will tend to, what economists call, a Pareto efficiency. Pareto efficiency is a state of the economy where resources are allocated most efficiently and any change to the state will not make someone happier without making someone else less happy. Economists Lionel McKenzie, Kenneth Arrow and Gérard Debreu amongst others proved this key result of analytical linkage between competitive markets and efficiency mathematically in the 1950s[1]. This result is sometimes known as the "First Fundamental Theorem of Welfare Economics." This relationship between free markets and Pareto efficiency creates a strong moral reason for free markets.

One can argue that in the real world, all the assumptions required for the markets to create efficient economic output may not exist. Hence, the stronger justification for economic liberty though comes from empirical evidence. Empirically it can be seen that higher per capita income in many countries has been fostered by liberal policies. The Heritage Foundation, a think tank, has produced an index to measure economic freedom across countries since 1995[2]. The index, called Index of Economic Freedom, co-published by The Wall Street Journal and The Heritage Foundation, measures economic freedom on various fronts including rule of law, government size, regulatory efficiency, and open markets[3]. A consolidated index is created with values between 0 and 100. A value of 100 represents the most economically free country. The graph below shows the relationship between economic

---

[1] Arrow, K. and Debreu, G. (1954). "Existence of an equilibrium for a competitive economy." Econometrica. Vol. 22.

[2] Details on the index are available at https://www.heritage.org/index

[3] Olson, R. (2014). "Using the index of economic freedom: A practical guide." Heritage.org [Web]. Retrieved from: https://www.heritage.org/international-economies/report/using-the-index-economic-freedom-practical-guide

freedom as measured by the index and the GDP (gross domestic product or the total output of the country) on a per capita basis (i.e. per person)[4]. Each point on the graph represents a country with the horizontal axis representing the Index of Economic Freedom[5] and the vertical axis representing the GDP per capita in US$. The graph is for the top 150 countries by GDP, where data is available. The relationship between the two is strong. All countries with an index value above 80 and most countries with an index value above 70 have GDP per capita more than $40,000. Other factors, like availability/scarcity of natural resources, explain some deviations like having high economic freedom but low GDP per capita. Also, some countries have just started on the journey of liberty and they will take more time to see the fruits of liberty.

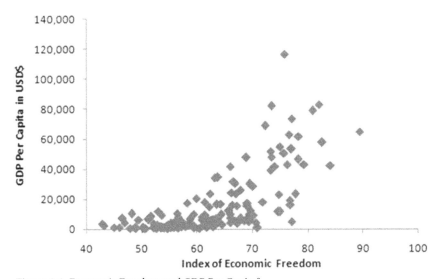

Figure 2.1. Economic Freedom and GDP Per Capita[6]
Data Sources: The Heritage Foundation[7] and World Bank[8]

---

[4] Some economists prefer using purchasing power adjusted GDP as prices are different in different countries. But I'm not adjusting for the purchasing power because of two reasons: 1. In a globalized world purchasing power adjustment is increasingly becoming meaningless as people can buy goods and services more or less from any country. 2. Purchasing power calculations are subjective as the adjustment factor will depend upon the basket of goods chosen to calculate the prices.

[5] Using the Index data published by The Heritage Foundation does not mean I automatically agree with all the views published by them.

[6] For the Index of Economic Freedom data is taken as of 2020. For GDP, the latest data available for each country is taken.

To demonstrate the relationship more clearly, the graph below shows the same data but for only the top thirty countries by GDP. Each bubble in the chart is a country. The size of the bubble reflects the size of the GDP of the country. Again the horizontal axis represents the Index of Economic Freedom and the vertical axis represents the GDP per capita in US$. Some of the bubbles are labeled with the name of the country they represent to give a better perspective.

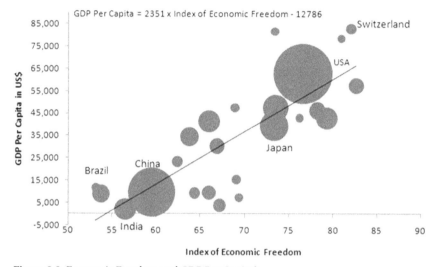

Figure 2.2. Economic Freedom and GDP Per Capita[9]
Data Sources: The Heritage Foundation[10] and The World Bank[11]

The relationship between economic freedom and GDP per person is unambiguous. Of course, there are several other factors that influence the GDP

[7] The Heritage Foundation (2020). *Index of economic freedom.* Heritage.org [Web]. Retrieved from: https://www.heritage.org/index/excel/2020/index2020_data.xls
[8] The World Bank (2020). *GDP per capita (current US$).* WorldBank.org [Web]. Retrieved from: https://data.worldbank.org/indicator/NY.GDP.PCAP.CD
[9] For the Index of Economic Freedom data is taken as of 2020. For GDP, the latest data available for each country is taken.
[10] The Heritage Foundation (2020). *Index of economic freedom.* Heritage.org [Web]. Retrieved from: https://www.heritage.org/index/excel/2020/index2020_data.xls.
[11] The World Bank (2020). *GDP per capita (current US$).* WorldBank.org [Web]. Retrieved from: https://data.worldbank.org/indicator/NY.GDP.PCAP.CD.

of a country, most important of them being natural resources and land per person. Nevertheless, economic freedom seems to be explaining a large part of the variance in income levels across countries. The relationship is systematically present across different sizes of countries and different population sizes. For every one point increase in the value of the index, the GDP per capita increases by $2,351. For the large economies, the relationship between economic freedom and GDP per capita seems to be stronger.

Even though the relationship between economic freedom and GDP per capita is indisputable, the correlation between the variables does not imply causation as it can be argued that countries that have become rich become economically free later rather than the other way round. But history shows that economic liberalization precedes high economic development. It can be seen in economies of various sizes and across different times, be it Classical Liberalism in 19th century Europe or Reaganomics in the USA or Thatcherism in the UK or economic liberalization in India in the 20th century. It is interesting to note that some of these economies have already started with a higher base for income and some have started with a lower base and increased significantly from there. This goes on to prove that liberal policies can work irrespective of the stage of the economy. Even when it comes to poverty alleviation, the free-market policy will yield better results than socialistic interventions, which only give temporary reprieve. For example, the best way we can help a poor farmer working on an infertile land is to provide him with opportunities to move out of farming. This will help him more than providing subsidies for seeds or fertilizers. We do not know what the alternative opportunities are for the farmer; but in a free and open market the farmer would be able to realize those opportunities himself. For that to happen, there should be freedom of choice and deep markets providing various opportunities. The prices and wages in these markets are a signal to the farmer as to which goods/skills are demanded by consumers. The farmer can then adapt accordingly. Not only does the market give more opportunities but it also gives signals for the farmer to choose a profession most useful for the society.

The effect of free-market economics is nowhere else as striking as in the UK, where it was first propounded by Adam Smith and then implemented by various regimes. The graph below shows how per capita incomes have evolved in the UK over the past six hundred years. As can be seen, although there has been a gradual growth in incomes, exponential growth started to happen in the 19th century and continued all the way into the 20th century, thus significantly increasing the living standards of innumerable citizens. Several factors including colonialism and industrialization can be claimed to be the reason for this. But the fact that the growth sustained even after the end of colonialism and the peak of industrial revolutions, suggests that economic policies are the ones fomenting it. The breakthrough seen in the UK has helped the whole world as they saw in the UK a proof of the concept of free-market policies. Japan, the US, and most western European countries emulated the free-market policies of the UK resulting in very positive outcomes for these economies.

Figure 2.3. UK Real GDP Per Capita (£)
Data Source: Bank of England[12]

A similar shift in growth is evident in developing economies that have adopted economically liberal policies more recently. For example, the graph below shows the growth in the per capita income of India from 1965 to 2018[13]. As is evident, there has been a quantitative shift in the growth rate post-1991, which is when economic liberalization was initiated in India. The average income growth from 1965 to 1991 has been a meager 1.86% p.a. whereas the average growth from 1992 to 2018 has been 4.92%. This puts into question the prolonged period of state-monitored economic management in India before 1991. Towards the start of the 1980s, Milton Friedman and his wife Rose Friedman authored and were part of a television series called *Free to Choose*,

---

[12] Bank of England (2020). *A mellenium of macroeconomic data.* BankofEngland.co.uk [Web]. Retrieved from: https://www.bankofengland.co.uk/-/media/boe/files/statistics/research-datasets/a-millennium-of-macroeconomic-data-for-the-uk.xlsx.

[13] The World Bank (2020). *GDP per capita (current US$).* WorldBank.org [Web]. Retrieved from: https://data.worldbank.org/indicator/NY.GDP.PCAP.CD.

covering various aspects of free-market economics. The series was updated again in 1990. In the series, he came down heavily upon the central planning and socialistic economic policies being implemented in India and recommended a move to open up the economy. Specifically, he argued that focusing only on a few industries like textiles and ignoring others has been very harmful to the economy. A year after the second edition of the series, India opened up its economy and dramatically unlocked the huge potential of the services industry. Specifically, India reduced tariffs on international trade, allowed automatic allowance of foreign investments in several sectors, and reduced the monopoly of government-owned businesses. This impacted India's GDP, per capita income, living standards, foreign exchange reserves, and her standing in the world.

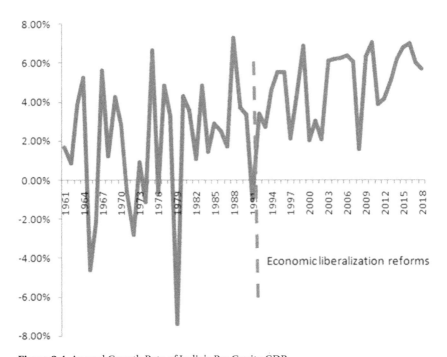

Figure 2.4. Annual Growth Rate of India's Per Capita GDP
Source: The World Bank[14]

---

[14] Ibid.

Another very interesting case study is that of Estonia. The Republic of Estonia was established in 1991 when it segregated from the former Soviet Republic. At the time of its independence, Estonia was considered just another poor Baltic country. Within a span of 25 years, by 2004, the country established itself as a rich country and a part of the European Union. This was achieved through a combination of implementing the rule of law, fiscal consolidation, and market freedom. On the Index of Economic Freedom Estonia is ranked 10th freest country in the world as of 2020. At the time of independence, Estonia's per capita GDP was less than that of Russia. As of 2020, Estonia's per capita GDP is more than double that of Russia. This is despite Estonia having no significant natural resources.

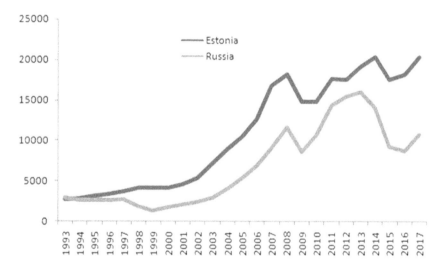

Figure 2.5. GDP Per Capita (Current US $)
Data Source: The World Bank[15]

In the western world, liberalization of the economy started with industrialization and continues till this date, punctuated briefly by interventionist policies. It can be argued that industrialization itself could have been sparked by a liberal environment. The counter-argument to complete free markets as advocated by interventionists is that the free market allows for price fluctuations which have a severe impact on employment rates

---

[15] Ibid.

and income of a wide set of people. Upon careful observation, we can conclude that most of the flaws in the current free-market policies are because of incomplete implementation of liberal policies like excessive control by the central bank or cronyism supporting corporations. I will look at some of these aspects in subsequent chapters. Nevertheless, there are certain issues that need to be addressed while implementing liberal economics like corporate corruption because of excessive greed emanating from market economics. Self-interest is integral to free markets, as it is the lubricant for the free market to function properly. The same self-interest pushing markets towards efficiency can push people and corporations towards corruption, I will look at why liberal economic policy need not necessarily imply giving preference to corporate interests in the chapter on the lacunas of current right-wing policies. The success of liberal policies will depend upon how this problem is solved with minimal intervention.

Before we discuss economic liberalization further, I want to briefly highlight why political liberty is equally important if not more important than economic liberty. In a politically liberal country, if the citizens feel that economically liberal policies will be beneficial to them, they can affect the changes without a revolution. If we were to believe economic liberalism benefits everyone and that citizens make rational decisions then political liberty should ensure economic liberalism. If the policies do not yield the expected benefits the citizens can roll back to socialism, protectionism, or other forms of non-liberal economic policies, again without a revolution. This is one of the reasons for the simultaneous growth of liberal economic policies and democracy around the world. The benefit of political liberty is the highest if citizens can participate directly in democracy, but even with indirect participation, citizens do hold enough power over the legislature to ensure the legislature forms policies that will benefit the citizens. One of the factors making democracies more efficient is the awareness of citizens. In many countries though, there is a gap in the economic awareness of citizens. The way to bridge this gap is through more discussions around economic policy and this book is an attempt towards that.

Having said that, from an empirical perspective, there are economies with limited political liberty but ample economic liberty that have shown significant economic progress and wealth. But these examples are only limited to countries with small geographic areas and such policies have not worked for large economies.

Liberal policies, where implemented, have not only helped increase economic growth but also have bridged wealth gaps by improving economic mobility, in contrast to the apprehensions of socialists like Karl Marx. It can be seen in the relationship between economic freedom and the share of income of the poor. The graph below shows the Index of Economic Freedom discussed earlier and the share of income of the bottom 10% of the economy. It shows the relationship for the thirty largest countries by GDP, excluding the Kingdom of Saudi Arabia (where data is not available). The relationship is positive, though not as strong as the relationship between economic freedom and GDP. Thus with increase in economic freedom not only does overall GDP increase but the gap in income between the rich and the poor also drops. Even if economic freedom has only a small impact on income equality, it will have a much bigger impact on the poor as the overall pie also increases with economic freedom.

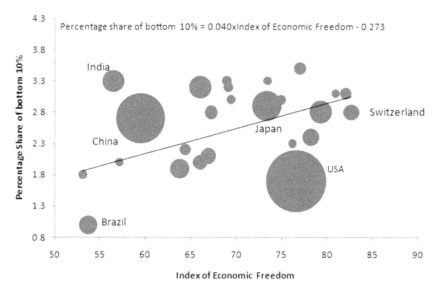

Figure 2.6. Economic Freedom and Share of Income of the Poor[16]
Data Sources: The Heritage Foundation[17] and The World Bank[18]

An argument against the free market is that the free market supports the corporations and the rich more and the effect on the poor is only a trickle-

---

[16] For the Index of Economic Freedom data as of 2020 is taken. For the income share of bottom 10% the latest data available for each country is taken.
[17] The Heritage Foundation (2020). *Index of economic freedom.* Heritage.org [Web]. Retrieved from: https://www.heritage.org/index/excel/2020/index2020_data.xls.
[18] The World Bank (2020). *Income share held by lowest 10%.* WorldBank.org [Web]. Retresived from: https://data.worldbank.org/indicator/SI.DST.FRST.10.

down. But, as seen in form empirical data, the free market helps the poor more. I want to call this the "trickle-up" effect of the free market. Trickle-up happens because the poor get more opportunities for income generation and also more avenues for spending in a free market. These contribute to both demand and supply in the economy and as a result helping the corporations to make more money. Also, even if the free market does not increase equality drastically, that is still fine as long as the poor are becoming richer because of the overall increase in incomes. For example, if in India the income share of bottom 10% people goes down from 3.3% to let us say 2%, but if overall GDP increases five times (on an inflation-adjusted basis), which is highly possible through increasing economic freedom, the poor in India are still better off by three times. Thus free markets could be the best way to help the poor, contrary to the apprehensions of socialists and interventionists.

Most socialists, starting with Karl Marx, looked at the world as a struggle between capital and labor. This has caused them to hypothesize that if capital were given more liberty then the laborer would be exploited. But it is ridiculous to presume that a capitalist wakes up every morning and says to herself "today I'm going to exploit x number of laborers." She just makes decisions that will maximize her payoff the same as what a laborer will do. In fact, most capitalists have been philanthropists. Also, today's laborer could be tomorrow's business owner and today's capitalist could give up her business because of the burdens of expenses and risks, and become a freelance professional tomorrow. That kind of mobility is possible when everyone has the liberty to do what she wants to do. Thus, I believe capital is highly overrated as a factor of production, so the class struggle between capital and labor is illusionary. This is one of the reasons I will not use the word "capitalism" and instead use the more generic words "free market", "open market" or "liberalism" as the capital market is only one of the several markets that operate in a free market economy.

Now that we have abandoned the divide of capitalist vs. laborer, the divide that remains is that of the wealthy and the not so wealthy. Economic liberty will help everyone, one with a lot of wealth or no wealth. On the margin, it should help the not so wealthy more because the motivation for them to become wealthier is higher. In a socialistic framework, this motivation is taken away. Easy access to financial and non-financial markets will support this motivation to materialize real wealth.

The reason I've countered Karl Marx's argument is that Marx is one of the most vociferous voices against free markets and most of the anti-free market rhetoric primarily originates from Marx. Currently, though, more than Marx, the threat to economic liberty comes from neo-Keynesians, who argue for higher spending by the government either for social justice or for economic stimulus. The Keynesian policy framework, propounded by Lord Keynes during the Great Depression, has been the first major deviation from liberal economics in the western world. Keynesian policies support the intervention of the government in the form of increased government spending for supporting the demand for goods and services in an economy. Post the financial crisis of this century, there has been a renewed interest in government intervention with a social justice overlay. Intervention by the government takes away liberties of people directly or indirectly and it is against the philosophy of free markets shaping the economy efficiently through an invisible hand. Spending by the government is the decision of a single person or a group of people, who may err sometime or the other however wise they might be. The invisible hand of markets on the other hand continuously corrects the economy through mechanisms of signaling. Another factor is that spending by the government will eventually come from the pockets of the citizens, thus leaving them with less income in the end. Even when, if at all, the government generates revenue through non-tax mechanisms (mostly through rents on land/resources) the ideal way to spend that would be to put that money back directly in the hands of the citizens, through some form of citizen's dividend.

Another threat to liberal policies comes from protectionists, who argue for priority to be given to domestic businesses/workforce. Protectionists are okay with free markets inside a country but are quite illiberal when it comes to international trade. This is a result of politics still being localized even though trade has become globalized. This is myopic as protecting the supply side (i.e. businesses and individuals producing goods and services) will be a disservice to the demand side (consumers looking to use those goods and services). Also, protectionism by one country can lead to counter protectionist measures by its trade partners. This process, known as trade war, will lead to an equilibrium that will be bad for all parties involved.

As protectionism is an imminent threat to liberalism, I want to elaborate a bit more on the benefits of international free trade. Let us take an example of two countries: Argentina and Bangladesh. (The use of the names Argentina and Bangladesh in this and subsequent examples is purely for illustration and should not be construed as a judgment on the current policies of these countries.) Bangladesh is competitive in producing all types of goods and services compared to Argentina. Let us say Argentina can make a good quality airplane at $100 million and Bangladesh can make a similar airplane at $80 million. Also, Argentina can manufacture a ship at $80 million and Bangladesh can manufacture a similar ship for $30 million. Each country needs a ship and also one airplane. Also, there is a constraint, that each country can produce only two units: one each of ship and airplane or two units either of ships or airplanes.

In a no-trade world, each country will produce one unit each of ship and airplane. The total cost of this endeavor will be $290 million ($180 million for Argentina and $110 million for Bangladesh).

Table 2.1. Cost of Each Country Producing One Unit Each of Ship and Airplane

Country	Cost per unit		Number of Units		Total cost
	Airplane	**Ship**	**Airplane**	**Ship**	
Argentina	$100	$80	1	1	$180
Bangladesh	$80	$30	1	1	$110
Total			2	2	**$290**

If, on the other hand, Argentina produces only airplanes and Bangladesh manufactures only ships then the total cost will be $260 million.

Table 2.2. Cost of Each Country Producing Goods Where it has Comparative Advantage

Country	Cost per unit		Number of Units		Total cost
	Airplane	**Ship**	**Airplane**	**Ship**	
Argentina	$100	$80	2	0	$200
Bangladesh	$80	$30	0	2	$60
Total			2	2	**$260**

This is lower than the cost of producing/manufacturing the goods individually. Now the only task that remains is that of trading goods with each other. Let us say, Bangladesh buys from Argentina one airplane at $105 million and sells to Argentina one ship for $70 million then it can be observed that each country will be procuring the goods it requires at a lower cost than the price at which it manufactures on its own.

Table 2.3. Cost of Each Country Producing Goods and Engaging in Trade

	Argentina	Bangladesh
Cost of production (A)	$200.00	$60.00
Import cost (B)	$70.00	$105.00

Export revenue (C)	$105.00	$70.00
Net outflow (A+B-C)	$165.00	$95.00

In this case, the total outflow (after accounting for revenue) is $165 million for Argentina and $95 million for Bangladesh, versus the cost of individual production of $180 million and $110 million respectively. Both countries benefit from the process of trade. This concept is called "the law of comparative advantage" and was developed by David Ricardo[19] in the early 19th century. The law of comparative advantage is one of the reasons why free trade benefits all. The law is applicable to individuals as much as to nations.

Other than the point that free trade benefits everyone, this example illustrates a couple of interesting points. Firstly, it highlights the point that in a world constrained by capital, labor, and resources, even countries that do not have an absolute competitive advantage, like Argentina in the above example, can benefit from trade. Secondly, as the name of the law suggests, countries should indulge in activities where they have comparative advantage vis-à-vis other activities. As Argentina can produce an airplane at only $20 million more than Bangladesh compared to $50 million for manufacturing the ship, it should focus on making airplanes rather than manufacturing ships. Similarly, even though Bangladesh is competitive in both making airplanes and building ships, it is better off making ships as it has a $50 million advantage. Lastly, this brings us to the point that countries should focus on areas where they have some advantage and build upon that to gain comparative advantage and acquire other goods and services through trade. So in the hypothetical example, Argentina and Bangladesh should build upon their strengths of building airplanes and ships respectively. And each of these countries can obtain other goods and services which they are not producing through trading with each other, rather than aiming to become self-reliant in all kinds of goods and services.

Evolution of economic policy frameworks

Principles of free trade have been adopted in the 19th century in England and then emulated elsewhere. There have been several economic crises in the 20th century and early 21st century. After each crisis, instead of going back to liberal policies, policymakers have adopted new forms of illiberalism. The first real threat to free trade and free markets came with the stock market crash of

---

[19] Gonner, E. C. K. and Ricardo, D. (1891). *Principles of Political Economy and Taxation.* United Kingdom: G. Bell and sons.

1929 and the subsequent economic depression called the Great Depression. After the Great Depression of the 1930s, Keynesianism, propounded by John Maynard Keynes, was adopted as a means to increase demand and reinvigorate the economy. Keynesianism argues for lowering taxes and increasing government expenditure when demand is low. Keynesians, i.e. followers of Keynes, assert that the "Aggregate Demand" in the economy does not automatically adjust to the "Aggregate Supply" and as a result government intervention is needed if demand for goods and services is low[20]. Keynes believed that the depression was caused because demand from private entities was not enough to match the supply, leading to a crash in prices and employment. What was a lack of liquidity or lack of depth in the market was, I believe wrongly, explained by new paradigms of Aggregate Demand and Aggregate Supply and their mismatch. Keynes argued that if aggregate demand by private entities does not match the aggregate supply, then the government should step in and bridge the gap. The flaws in this framework came to light over time.

Prolonged use of interventionist measures propounded by Keynes, has led to the stagflation (simultaneous stagnation and inflation) of the 1970s and 80s. The logical flaws in Keynes' theory became bare in this period. This resulted in the adoption of a new economic theory - monetarism. Monetarism argues for using money supply (amount of money circulating in the economy) to control the growth of the economy and inflation. Monetarism was initially propounded by Milton Friedman as a tool for controlling inflation. Monetary economists rightly identified that managing the economy through government spending will have unforeseen side effects. Monetarism put the onus of economic management, especially the management of inflation, on the central banks. Monetarism, coupled with a free market, has been the main policy framework in the western world until now (i.e. 2020). I believe, in contrast to several free-market proponents including Milton Friedman, that monetarism is the wrong medicine for the problem. Although the prescriptions of Keynes and Friedman are different, the methodology of Friedman is still Keynesian. While Keynesianism resulted in the stagflation of the 1970s and 1980s, monetarism especially in the USA has resulted in two bubbles and subsequent busts in 2000 (internet bubble) and 2008 (mortgage credit bubble). The bubbles and busts can be explained by the fact that the government's hand in terms of the money supply was being used to guide the economy rather than the invisible hand of markets. In other words, the

---

[20] Keynes, J. M. (1936). *The general theory of employment, interest and money*. New York City: Harcourt, Brace.

government was monopolizing money. The impact of these two bubbles was so big that the effect was felt across the world. Monetarism didn't stop after the crisis and it is still being used as a dominant policy framework as of 2020, including the development of a new framework of Modern Monetary Theory. We may be heading towards another crisis, which we will know only after it breaks out. Going further back in history, monetarists themselves argue that the great depression of the 1930s has been caused by inappropriate use of monetary policy. Thus they admit that policymakers can err while using monetary policy causing catastrophic results. While Milton Friedman passionately argues for free markets everywhere, it is a pity that he fails to see the elephant in the room - monopolization of money by the government. We will examine these issues more carefully in the chapter on money.

After the great recession of 2008, protectionism, coupled with neo-Keynesianism, has gained currency. I believe the negative effects of protectionism are nigh upon us. Protectionists believe that domestic businesses should be supported by discouraging competition from foreign businesses through the use of import restrictions and tariffs. This is contrary to economic logic that, if a country can produce certain goods at a very low cost, there is no need for other countries to replicate the effort. Unfortunately, as nations look at their own interests, they will end up in a bad equilibrium (equilibrium is a stable but not necessarily most productive state of the economy), although there always exists a good equilibrium. I will look at this in detail in the chapter on the lacunas of right-wing policies.

Along with protectionism, neo-Keynesianism is another threat to liberal economics currently. Proponents of neo-Keynesianism support government intervention in supporting the economy when there is a downturn. They advocate steps like stimulus packages to certain segments of the economy, bailing out of companies, etc. This logic is flawed on two fronts. Firstly, if the government supports businesses and certain segments of the economy, there will be an incentive for businesses to be inefficient and take excessive risks. Secondly, any support to a particular segment of the economy has to come from taxation on the rest of the economy. This is unjust and also an inefficient way of wealth distribution. Lastly, the act of sectors of the economy or businesses going bust is not a problem but a solution to inefficiencies. Inefficient companies get weeded out in an economic downturn thus making the recovery faster.

The reason I have digressed from the topic of economic liberty and taken a brief jaunt in the history of economic theory is to illustrate the fact that any kind of intervention by the government will eventually lead to unintended side effects. Each of the above illiberal sets of policies has led to the subsequent crisis and none of them can remain a long-term policymaking framework. Although I use a strong word – illiberal, I want to qualify that by saying that I use it only with the meaning of "not being completely defined by the free market framework." The intention of policymakers at the time of implementing these policies might have been virtuous; they might have genuinely believed that these policy frameworks to be the solutions to the prevalent problems. We are able to judge their effectiveness properly only because of hindsight, not because we are smarter or more passionate about finding the solution.

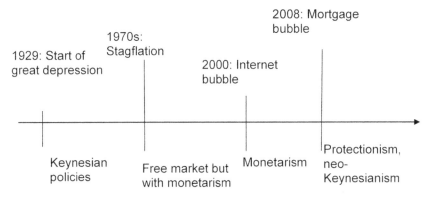

Figure 2.7. Evolution of Various Economic Policy Frameworks in the Last 100 Years

So after rejecting Keynesianism, monetarism, and protectionism, what does an economically liberal policy framework entail? To start with the basics, rule of law should be established and life and private property should be protected from appropriation by others or by the state itself. Every person should be allowed to pursue a profession as per her preferences and her motivations should not be discouraged through high taxes. There are two parts to this. Firstly, there should be minimal restrictions on choosing a profession or starting a business. Especially there should not be any licensing of businesses and regulatory requirements to run businesses should be low. Secondly, income generated because of the contribution of labor (either to own profession, own business, or someone else's business) should not be taxed highly. One's body and mind are the first set of properties that one owns and taxing their use goes against the principles of liberty. It may be necessary to levy certain taxes as the government also provides an environment conducive to make money from physical or mental labor, but that has to be minimal.

Freedom of doing business also involves ease of raising and using capital through various instruments (equity, debt, hybrid instruments, etc.). The restrictions on raising money through public and private money/capital markets should be minimal. Historically the restrictions on such activities are high to protect the small investor. Today even a small investor is aware of the risks of investment and can make a judgment based on merits and expected rewards. Thus the role of regulations in capital markets is diminishing. The main role of regulation should be limited to reducing information asymmetry and making all parties involved aware of the risks and be on the same footing in terms of information availability.

In addition to internal freedoms, labor, capital (money), goods, and services should be allowed to move freely without the country. That means liberalizing international trade and investment. Restrictions on foreign trade and foreign investments should be eliminated. Duties/tariffs on imports and exports should be minimal.

Apart from these basic tenets, the overarching principle is that there should be a minimal intervention in economic activities from the state. The state should only take care of a few functions with minimal spending. To support free markets, where possible, monopolies especially through rent seeking on land or government approval should be busted. Financial markets, including money and currency markets, and non-financial markets should be allowed to operate freely. Liberties should be curtailed only to prevent entities from infringing upon the rights of others.

The reason liberal economics strongly advocate minimum government intervention is that no one, including the government, has complete knowledge to make perfect decisions. Whereas in a free market where each agent acts freely, the market forces ensure that an efficient solution is achieved. An analogy is that of molecules in an ideal gas, which moves randomly without any coordinated planning, but when they are trapped inside a ball, they put equal pressure on all sides and ensure the ball achieves a perfect spherical shape. Similarly, agents in the free market might act completely randomly with their own personal goals in mind, but that achieves a collective efficiency, which cannot be replicated using central planning, especially in the face of several uncertainties coming from exogenous forces, nature, technology, etc.

The liberty accorded to individuals not only increases competition and efficiency in the short term but also encourages progress through the development of new ideas in the long term. These two outcomes are the result of a deep human need to excel, to which liberty acts as a catalyst. In a world with maximum liberty, the businessman excels in creating maximum value, the craftsman excels in creating the best products from resources available, the scientist excels at arriving at the most promising discoveries, etc. Thus liberty helps in achieving economic efficiency in the present and also progress in the future. I'm not stating anything new but reiterating what Adam Smith and other early economists have established in the 18th and 19th centuries. The details of the implementation will of course change as times have changed and we have more experience with economic policies now.

Am I then asking for states to blindly open up markets, and reduce spending and taxes? Mostly yes. Should the weak also be made to compete in a Darwinian economic world driven by 'the survival of the fittest' dictum? Definitely not. Unlike social and political liberties, economic liberties do not stand merely on a moral or natural justice ground. Economic liberties also ensure social justice and prosperity for everyone. If that does not happen, we need to relook at and tweak the policy framework. I'm not looking at liberty only purely from a radical individualistic view of man, although that is a primary justification for liberty. I view economic liberty as being not only consistent with natural liberties the man is born with, but it is also a pragmatic policy for achieving prosperity for all.

Chapter 3

On the lacunas of right-wing policies

The primary advocates of free-market policies across the world are right wing, sometimes also called conservative, political parties. They also usually advocate minimal government spending and low taxation. Even though not all right-wing/conservative parties have the same economic policy, they operate on similar broad strokes. The liberal economic policies described earlier should be in natural agreement with the right-wing economic policies. That is true in general, but there are some specific points where I see differences both in the principles and the details. I have called these differences 'lacunas' in the title of this chapter; the conservatives themselves might be seeing these differences as strengths of their political philosophy. Nevertheless, it is important to highlight these differences. I do not intend to do the same exercise with left-wing policies, as the differences between left-wing policies and the economic policies I'm advocating here are quite obvious. On the points where there are some similarities between the two, I will be open in pointing them out in subsequent chapters.

I will be using the words "right-wing" and "conservative" interchangeably. There is no universally accepted definition of what constitutes right-wing/conservative economic policy framework, so some people may not consider some of the ideas I'm countering in this chapter as right-wing/conservative ideas. But it should be noted that I'm opposing certain economic ideas, which I think are flawed, and not any particular group as such. I definitely do not want this chapter to be a political statement and I'm only listing out the differences to bring out key points of liberalism. In this chapter, I will also examine a few areas where the free market framework itself could fail, questioning some of the libertarian policies as well.

The main areas where current right wing (and other free markets proponents) have a conflict with the principles espoused in this book include:

- Conservatism does not allow for rational liberalism

- Right-wing is overtly corporate-friendly

- Aggressive profit-seeking by corporations will drain resources fast and this fact is not addressed appropriately by conservatives

- Conservatives are turning into protectionists

- Benefits of free markets are not reaching the grassroots and this is not critically examined by conservatives and even libertarians

- Free markets ignore transitional phases; which can have an irreversible effect on individuals

- Conservatives equate liberty exclusively to property rights

- Right-wing parties do not fully support social and political liberties

Conservatism does not allow for rational liberalism

My first objection to prevalent conservative policies comes from the fact that conservatives treat economic liberty as an ideal because they see it as a tradition being followed for centuries. They do not derive economic liberalism from the principles of moral philosophy or from the pragmatic approach of economics. To conservatives, economic liberty is sort of an end in itself. The logic they use to support economic liberty is that human knowledge is limited and conventions evolved overtime to ensure the best outcome is achieved for humans and thus they have to be adhered to without many rationalizations. To my mind, the argument is flawed because even if established conventions give the best outcome, there is nothing wrong in examining them rationally from time to time.

The conservative movement in the West arose as a counterforce to the collectivism advocated by left-liberals post World War II. Thus their opposition to large government spending on social welfare is also an antithesis of socialism, which was gaining popularity in the 1950s. To counter the post-war socialistic trends, conservatives wanted to go back to, what they believed, the long-established tradition of individualism and entailing economic freedom of the individual.

Where conservatives derive their economic framework from tradition, several liberals/libertarians and I derive it from the principle of the natural liberty of man and rational economic theories established in the last 200 odd years. Although it is true that man was free for a long time before the establishment of nation-states, natural liberty of man, as we understand it today, is not established by a tradition but by philosophical and moral arguments starting with philosophers in ancient civilizations, but more recently popularized by John Locke in the 17th century. Similarly, rational economic theories starting with the publication of *The Wealth of Nations* have supported economic liberty using logical and at times, mathematical arguments. As conservatives do not derive their worldview from such rational thought processes, they are less flexible in adapting to changes in the environment and are usually opposed to new ideas.

True liberalism is guided by principles of accepting change and innovation coming from the free human spirit. It welcomes new ideas from every strand of ideology, leading to the evolution of society and its rules. The growth and evolution of the society that liberalism envisages is spontaneous and maybe even haphazard at times. This is in contrast to the conservative principle of sticking to stable morals and rules established by tradition. These are the same sentiments echoed by F. A. Hayek, Nobel laureate in economics, in his postscript of *The Constitution of Liberty*[1]. The postscript was aptly titled "Why I am not a conservative."

These differences are not just restricted to the philosophical or moral realm, but show up in practical aspects as well. Economic liberalism derived from the rational application of economic theory and moral philosophy can be a fluid policy framework, continuously changing with changing times. Conservatism, on the other hand, by definition resists change. For example, if at any stage there is a conflict between economic liberalism and the goal of universal prosperity, I would not be reluctant to sway against economic liberty. In other words, to me letting someone live in abject poverty is much more immoral than denying someone already prosperous of her economic liberties. Not all conservatives may take a similar stand. On similar lines, if evidence suggests that central planning might be better in certain aspects of economic activity in terms of reaching efficiency and equity, then I would advocate for the same. These deviations from full economic liberty are some of the ideas that I will be discussing in subsequent chapters, especially in the chapter on universal basic income.

Right wing is overtly corporate-friendly

Right-wing parties equate economic liberty usually with minimal restrictions on corporate activities, including lower corporate tax. This is a flawed extension of the concept of freedom accorded to individuals. I call this "corporatism" rather than economic liberalism or libertarianism. Economic liberalism supports the liberty of all entities and does not give corporates a preferential treatment. I'll go one step ahead and say - when it comes to rights and liberties, individual liberties have to be prioritized over corporate liberties because corporations themselves are created by a legal structure and are not natural entities. Thus when there is a conflict with regards to the freedom of

---

[1] Hayek, F. A. (1960). *The constitution of liberty*. Chicago: University of Chicago Press.

individuals versus corporate freedom, the first one should take precedence. Similarly, when there is a conflict between the rights of society on natural resources versus corporate activity involving consuming those resources, the first one should take priority. Some conservatives may give higher priority to individual rights and the rights of the society on natural resources, but usually, most right-wing parties give equal rights to corporate entities if not more. This arises from the misconception that corporate entities derive their rights naturally from the rights of individuals. This misconception can lead to the exploitation of employees, customers, and natural resources by corporate entities. Corporations and other legal persons are fundamentally different from natural persons (humans), as they exist primarily to serve humanity and are established by a legal framework. Another significant difference is the principle of limited liability accorded to corporations. Because of these reasons, one could think of several fundamental rights that can be only applicable to natural persons. Thus the right of full economic liberty accorded to natural persons is not completely transferable to corporations formed by them. Corporations also enjoy rights, which have to be subservient to the rights of individuals. Where there is no conflict between these two, I would argue for full freedom of corporations to make their business decisions and act upon them.

The origin of legal entities in the western world can be traced to the Christian Church establishing the concept of "persona ficta", in the middle ages, to enable monasteries to have independent existence and rights, including the right to own property. This ensured certain restrictions on monks (like living in poverty) are not violated, at the same time monasteries can manage the required infrastructure. The concept was further extended to business enterprises during the industrial revolution with additional rights like the right to enter into contracts and the right to sue or be sued. It should be recognized that all these rights are bestowed upon the legal entities by society. Hence in the time of conflict between the rights of the two of them (legal entities, i.e. corporations and society) the rights of society take precedence.

Two areas where these conflicts are very clear are monopolization and natural resource hoarding/exploitation by corporations. Monopolization is the chief antagonist of competitive markets, yet it is inevitable in free-market economies, largely because of certain economies of scale and the stochastic nature of business growth. Monopolies are bad for customers and also they restrict the use of some properties (intellectual/digital/real), leading to inefficiencies for the whole economy. North American leaders, in the progressive era (early 20th century), have identified this early on and implemented anti-monopoly laws (or anti-trust laws as they are called in the US). These reforms have ushered in a new era of competition in the USA, other economies followed suit.

Conservatives do not always support antitrust legislation and ensuing actions on corporations. This is in a way justified as long as in the long run competitive forces can counter monopolization. But where liberties of others are getting curbed through cartelization or exclusive rights on natural resources, antitrust laws should bust them. Such monopolization becomes a block for competition and there is a case for some intervention. I will leave it to the reader to learn specific cases where the legal antitrust framework is necessary to curtail malpractices of corporations, but some examples are:

- Collusion amongst various players to manage price (cartelization)

- Charging low price with the intention to kill competition (predatory pricing)

- Making buying of one product contingent on buying another product (tying)

- Boycotting a certain set of customers or vendors

- Discriminatory pricing: selling products at different prices to different customers[2]

The other area where conservatives usually are blindsided in favor of corporations is regarding externalities generated by corporations. Briefly put, externalities are effects of economic activity on people/land who are not involved in the activity directly. Externalities can be positive or negative. For example, the positive externality of building a road could be the development of towns the road passes through. Negative externality of the road could be the pollution caused by the vehicles going on the road. Externalities are tough to measure and monitor. As a result, corporations and the groups supporting them can conveniently ignore them. Right-wing parties tend to ignore the negative externalities, especially pollution, coming out of economic activity. They sometimes do acknowledge positive externalities, for example, some conservatives advocate giving incentives to corporations for setting up factories or facilities in particular states/municipalities to promote employment and development in that area. Denial of global warming is an extreme case of this corporate bias in conservatives.

---

[2] Not all discriminatory pricing is anti-competitive. For example giving discounts to students is a valid practice to increase the market for a product or a service. Discriminatory pricing with the intention of eliminating competition is bad for free-markets.

Aggressive profit seeking by corporations will drain natural resources fast

Intergenerational markets are practically non-existent in the current world. For example, we do not get paid by our kids for saving petroleum for them. As a result, there is no incentive for economic activities to save natural resources for future generations. Even within a generation, markets are not deep enough to know the long-term consequences of natural resource draining. This is a market failure that can be addressed only through some intervention or regulation.

Forests, groundwater, petroleum are a few examples where enough exploitation has already happened and we are seeing the consequences. Draining of a natural resource need not come only from large corporations but also individuals and the government, but large scale coordinated draining can happen only by large corporations, which are, rightfully, trying to optimize the current profit. Land and natural resources are the property of society. Individuals, governments, and corporations have appropriated them for vested use. Economic activity cannot progress without the use of natural resources. But quick and inefficient use of resources can create severe problems in the future. This can be addressed through some form of regulation.

There are several ways in which regulation of natural resource usage can be done. One way is to make all natural resources public and the government can extract as much as is required. The second way is to put a cap on resource usage by corporations. Thirdly, there could be a tax on the extraction of resources, called severance tax or stumpage tax. The first option is obviously very undesirable as leaving the decision making on allocations to the government can lead to inefficient decisions. An overall cap on extraction or a tax could be of help. The problem with the cap is that, in case excess resources are required at any point in time, there is no market-driven way to extract them. Taxing extraction instead of capping it can be a more market-oriented approach. Taxing can also generate additional money for the society. Some communities have decided to put this tax in an endowment for the future when the extraction will stop. I will discuss the severance tax further in the chapter on taxation.

Conservatives are turning into protectionists

Any form of control on trade is against the principles of economic liberty. We have seen in the chapter on liberty that countries benefit by focusing on the goods and services where they have competitive advantage and trade with other countries for obtaining other goods and services. But recently, especially after the crisis of 2008, several conservative groups have been advocating protectionist policies like import substitutions, tariffs, and barriers to trade and labor. It is a well-established fact that free trade benefits all the countries involved, but because of siloed decision-making, individual countries are forced to choose in such a way that the outcome is not optimal for the countries as a group. Protectionists in various countries argue that their country should protect a variety of industries from external forces, even if the country does not have any comparative advantage in certain industries. Part of the reason is to please their local constituency, but another important reason is the siloed decision-making leading to "prisoner's dilemma".

Prisoner's dilemma is a situation where two prisoners (let's say Alice and Bob) are locked in separate cells and are being interrogated separately. The investigators can prove their crimes only if one or both of them give evidence against the other. Alice is offered a deal where if she confesses and gives evidence against Bob, she will be let go and Bob will be given a sentence of five years. A similar deal is given to Bob. If neither defects, both of them will be given a sentence of one year on a lesser charge. If both of them defect, each will be given a sentence of two years. If the prisoners want their best outcomes they will cooperate with each other and not give evidence against the other thus both of them getting a lower sentence. But since they are kept in separate cells and each of them is trying to maximize his/her own benefit, both of the prisoners will have an incentive to defect.

A similar situation can be imagined in the case of international trade where each country is making a decision on whether to impose trade tariffs or not. The following table gives a stylized description of the tariff choices of two countries and the economic impact of the decisions. These decisions and outcomes are quoted purely for example; in the real world, the relationships are much more complex. Nevertheless, the example illustrates the negative effects of trade restrictions.

Table 3.1. Prisoner's Dilemma Applied to International Trade

		The decision of the US	
		The US imposes trade tariffs	The US does not impose trade tariffs
The decision of China	China Imposes trade tariffs	**Scenario A** Both countries lose $50B each	**Scenario B** The US loses $100B. China gains $75B
	China does not impose trade tariffs	**Scenario C** China loses $100B. The US gains $75B	**Scenario D** Both countries gain $50B each

From the perspective of China, if it assumes that the US will impose trade tariffs, it is exposed to Scenarios A and C. It is logical that China chooses to impose trade tariffs, as Scenario A is more advantageous to the country than Scenario C. If China assumes the US will not impose trade tariffs, then it is exposed to Scenarios B and D. Even in that case, China is incentivized to impose tariffs as Scenario B is better than D for itself. Similarly, the US will also make the choice of imposing trade tariffs, irrespective of whether it assumes China to impose trade tariffs or not. Imposing tariffs is what economists call a "dominant strategy". Thus in an endeavor to avoid scenarios C and B, the countries will end up in Scenario A, which is the worst scenario for both of them put together and also individually for each country it is worse than Scenario D.

This suboptimal decision-making results in protectionism being favored by each of the countries. Even though this is a stylized example, real-world scenarios also exhibit similar behavior. So how do we come out of this suboptimality? The good news is that unlike in the case of prisoners, decision-makers in each country are not locked up in cells, but are free to interact and collaborate. Each country can be more transparent about its options and constraints with the other country and they can communicate with each other to see that Scenario D is the best option for them. Trade summits and international trade organizations could facilitate this exchange of information.

Another factor that drives protectionism is the logic that self-reliance is important for national security. Some people argue that at least for defense goods, food, and certain key sectors like financial services, a nation should build self-reliance. I want to specifically counter the arguments in favor of self-reliance in the manufacturing of defense goods and food production. In fact, I would argue the other way round saying that relying only on one's own resources and technology can put the country in an inferior position. For the best national security, the country needs the best arms and technology from whichever part they originate. Not relying on other countries might put the country in greater danger. Diversifying trading partners and not relying on a small group of partners can mitigate the national security risk of reliance on external vendors. Similarly, for food security, over-reliance on internal production can put the country at risk of natural disruptions. I'm not saying that a country should not produce defense goods and food internally. I'm only saying that it should fulfill all the defense and food requirements completely internally, only if it is most competitive in doing so, compared to all other economic activities it can undertake.

Protectionism has become popular after 2008 because politics has remained localized while economic activities have become increasingly globalized. It has become easier for local politicians to blame external forces for the negative effects of the economic downturn. What the politicians and policymakers miss out is that protectionism will put the local consumers at a disadvantage while pandering to the local producers of goods and services. This will backfire at some stage.

Benefits of free markets are not reaching the grassroots

The efficiency of the free market is a theoretical concept, in practice though, the advantages of free-market policies need not percolate to all parts of the society. Market failures caused by frictions in the economy and geographical considerations (immobility of factors) prevent the benefits of the free market from reaching certain lower strata of the society. This problem is not completely addressed by conservatives. A good way to address these problems is through government intervention in developing infrastructure, to reduce the cost of market reach. This ensures that there is no sector-specific intervention leading to inefficient allocations at the same time the broader society is included in the market economy. Physical and digital infrastructure help markets to reach various parts of society. Two main parts of physical infrastructure that are required for efficient markets are transportation infrastructure and public spaces for trading/exchanging physical goods.

Digital infrastructure is already helping everyone to connect to markets hitherto inaccessible by certain segments. As communication infrastructure is becoming cheaper by the day, the role of government intervention is limited in this. Several markets that do not require physical presence, like financial services, can be directly accessible through digital means. Educating citizens on the use of these platforms/markets is the only missing piece of the puzzle. That is where there is some limited role of the government. In other words, the government can step in to reduce information asymmetry in various segments of society for accessing the markets.

Some services like health care require special infrastructure (ambulances, hospitals with beds, labs, etc.). As a result, the cost of delivery of these services to all parts of society can be very high. As some of these services are essential for sustenance, leaving everything to market forces can be disastrous. The government can intervene where there is a market failure in such services, at the same time keeping intervention limited. One extreme of the government monopolizing health care is bad, at the same time leaving everyone, including the poor, to private healthcare, which could become very expensive is also bad. Encouraging citizens to take insurance and subsidizing infrastructure for healthcare could be a middle ground.

Another area where market failure is possible in some societies is the field of education. Most libertarians and conservatives argue that the public education system is inefficient and a completely free market-driven education system is most desirable. Although in principle that is true, education is a long gestation investment and sometimes the impact is intergenerational. As a result, some citizens may not be willing or cannot afford to pay the fair price of education, leading to a market failure. This is where government intervention is advocated by educationalists. Free market proponents take the example of the US public education system to highlight the hypothesis that public education has led to deterioration in the quality of school education, as opposed to the high quality of higher education in the US, which is allowed to operate competitively. A via media between government-provided education and a complete non-interventionist approach towards education is the government giving education vouchers for kids, which can be used for education in a preferred school, thus keeping the competition alive. I'm not going deeper here (i.e. in the cases of healthcare and education), as the specific failure and the specific solution will change from society to society. There are several well-elaborated liberal views on the topic, which the reader is free to pore upon and form his or her own opinion.

Free markets ignore transitional phases

Free market policies rely heavily on a theory called "General equilibrium theory". Léon Walras first propounded general equilibrium theory in the 19th century. The theory says that in the long run markets adjust in such a way that supply matches demand for all components of the market. Unlike equilibrium in a single market, general equilibrium involves equilibrium across several markets including goods, services, money, capital, labor, etc. Each of these individual markets interacts with other markets to form a network and attain stability. Most economic theories, especially the ones that argue that the free market allocates resources efficiently, are derived using the general equilibrium framework as the background. The problem with this framework though is that it applies only in the long run. Even Walras himself concedes that the markets may be only continuously moving towards the equilibrium without ever actually achieving it- "The market is like a lake agitated by the wind, where the water is incessantly seeking its level without ever reaching it."[3] While the market is striving to achieve general equilibrium, there will be transitional phases where there could be excess supply or excess demand. Market forces like price feedback etc. ensure that these excesses are corrected. But the correction will take time and that can create distress in certain parts of the economy, especially when there are tectonic shifts in external factors like

---

[3] Walras, L. (2013). *Elements of pure economics.* United Kingdom: Taylor & Francis. Page 380.

technological changes, rapid climate change, or geopolitical events. Most free-market proponents including conservatives and libertarians broadly underplay the significance of the transitional phases.

In the previous chapter, I have asserted that if a farmer is not able to find enough opportunities in farming, for reasons not under his control, he should move to other more fetching occupations. I concede that that is a simplistic statement. The glitch with that solution is that to move to another occupation, the farmer will have to develop new skills. This does not happen overnight and he may not have the resources to do the same. This is a transitory phase but a very important one for the farmer and by extension the society.

The solution to this problem is rather tricky. An interventionist approach like the state providing skill development or forcefully placing him in alternative vocation through subsidies or coercion would only create more distortions. A non-distortionary way of providing support to the poorer section while the market tends towards equilibrium is to give them sustenance income. Such guaranteed income schemes or universal basic income schemes might at first seem quite opposite to free-market policies and tending towards socialism, but when we think about it deeply, they are quite consistent with the liberal framework I have been discussing. These schemes are in a way dividends the citizens earn from society for sharing resources with others. I will deliberate further on this topic in the chapter on universal basic income.

Conservatives equate liberty to property rights

Several conservatives and even some libertarians give high importance to property rights to the extent that they equate freedom to the right to own property. The right to own property is a very important factor of liberty. Firstly, the right to property protects citizens from the excesses of government, and secondly, it provides a stable environment to build businesses. But freedom expressed only as a right to property is a limited definition of freedom. Other rights, including freedom of movement, occupation, expression, etc., are equally important. Looking at liberty only from the lens of property rights restricts the full force of liberty.

Also, the right to property is not absolute, especially when the property in question is land (just to clarify the word land also includes all the natural resources that come with land). Land has been violently acquired in the past. So today's landowners are in a way beneficiaries of violence of the past. I'm not arguing for redistribution of land, but as land and society are very closely linked, the holding of land should come with some responsibilities. One of them being the responsibility of not undertaking any activity with a negative impact on the surrounding environment (water mining is an example, which can drain groundwater from all the surrounding areas as well). Another key aspect to holding land is to provide right of way, as blocking right of way could interfere with the freedom of movement of others. Lastly, as a large portion of the value of land comes from society around the land, there is a moral justification for property tax levied on land holding. Most conservatives ignore some of these finer nuances of land holding. We will look at some of these issues in more detail in subsequent chapters.

Right-wing parties do not fully support social and political liberties

I will only briefly touch upon this topic, as I don't want to make this book a book on politics. Some right-wing parties usually do not fully support social and political freedoms. Even if some right-wing parties are not against social or political liberties, they do not explicitly champion them. This may have come about because of historic reasons, as conservatives emerged from a counter-movement to communism. This observation may not be true for all right-wing groups, but where it is true I like to point out that economic liberties cannot stand on their own - they need the background of social and political liberties to bloom fully. As argued in the previous chapter, economic liberty derives its moral justification from man's freedom in all aspects of life. Even purely from a practical economic standpoint, political and social freedoms attract talents and global investments into the economy. Thus providing only economic freedoms and curtailing other forms of freedom is a gap in the policies of some right-wing groups.

To sum up, the individual centric liberal economic policy that I would like to propound in the book goes contrary to certain aspects of the current right-wing/conservative principles. The main point of contention is that I argue that the rights of individuals should take precedence over the rights of corporations and those of the state. Conservatives, on the other hand, give high precedence to corporate rights. Another point is that, when it comes to public goods (like natural resources) and externalities, the rights of the collective society take precedence over the rights of individuals. Conservatives, on the other hand, do not care so much about the exploitation of natural resources and externalities caused by businesses. Some of these points of differences have an effect on how liberal economic policies are implemented as we see in detail in the subsequent chapters.

Part 2: Core

Chapter 4

On the role of government

I heartily accept the motto, –That government is best which governs least; and I should like to see it acted up to more rapidly and systematically.[1]

- Henry David Thoreau

The intervention of the government in the economy in any form usually leads to inefficiencies as the government consists of a limited number of people and they do not have all the information required for making perfect decisions. This logic is applicable for any kind of governance, but more relevant for decisions on economic policies, as economics connects several individuals and corporate entities in an intricate network. F. A. Hayek gave a beautiful exposition on the information gap in his Nobel Prize lecture, aptly titled "The pretence of knowledge."[2] There are three types of limitations that the government faces because of which they cannot make the most optimal decisions. One, they are not present everywhere, so they will not have the localized and minute price and value information, which the market has. Secondly, when the price or value of a certain good or service changes, it affects the behavior of entities and also the prices of other goods and services. This effect is only observable in a dynamic market and cannot be captured in static information. Thirdly, it is computationally not possible to calculate all outcomes of all decisions to come up with the most optimal decision. Hence a large part of economic activity should be left to the markets, which give rise to spontaneous order, rather than leaving it to a central entity like the government. The information gap that the government faces is deeply structural and cannot be cured by more technology or other means.

Smaller role of government is also in line with the minimal taxation, as taxation will directly control the size of government expenditure. I will get into the details of taxation in the subsequent chapter. The smallest possible

---

[1] Thoreau, H. D. (2016). *Civil Disobedience*. United States: Xist Publishing. Page 1.
[2] Hayek, F. A. (1974). "The pretence of knowledge - Prize Lecture." NobelPirze.org [Web]. Retrieved from: https://www.nobelprize.org/prizes/economic-sciences/1974/hayek/lecture/.

government in liberal political science is sometimes referred to as "Nachtwächterstaat" or "nightwatchman state". The idea is that the state should act like a nightwatchman protecting the rights of the citizenry without interfering in any of the citizenry's activities. In actuality, government expenditure is increasing across the world (in absolute terms and also more importantly, as a percentage of GDP. The graph below shows the total government expenditure of the world as a percentage of GDP has gone up significantly in the fifty years. This is a testament to the fact that governments get used to spending and any increase in spending is very tough to roll back.

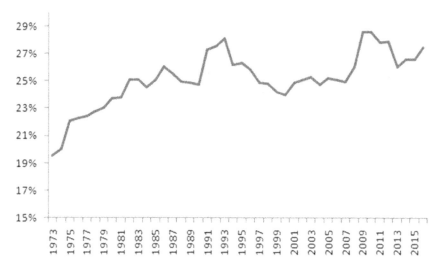

Figure 4.1. Central Government Expenditure of the World as a Percentage of GDP
Source: Our World in Data[3]

Although in this chapter, I refer to the role of the government, it is understood that the government is not a monolithic entity. There are several arms of the government, like the executive, legislative, and judicial branches. Also, in larger countries, there is a hierarchy of the government in terms of central, state, and municipal governments. The autonomy of each of these levels of government also keeps varying. It is desired that the local

---

[3] Our World in Data (2017). *Central government expenditure as share of GDP*. OurWorldinData.org [Web]. Retrieved from: https://ourworldindata.org/grapher/total-gov-expenditure-gdp-wdi.

government (i.e. state or municipal) gets greater autonomy, to perform governmental activities more efficiently. This is because the local government will have more information about local issues and also individuals will have more electoral power on local governments. The majority of the spending, in any case, will have to happen at the local level. I will discuss these issues in the chapter on decentralization.

Not only the size of intervention but also the nature of the intervention is important. I will critically examine which areas the government can intervene without curtailing freedoms and distorting the markets. The axiom with which I will work is that the government will have to intervene when markets and entities in the market cannot effectively serve a certain purpose essential for the smooth running of society. These areas are called market failures. There are several reasons for a market failure, I will classify these into three categories: public goods, regulations, and welfare. Public goods are commodities and services provided by an entity where the total benefit to the society is higher or lower than (but not equal to) the price of the goods or service in the market. Essentially, these are goods and services that impact the society at large without anyone directly paying the full cost. Another area is where the market, because of the self-interest of the participants, does not regulate itself properly. This is where external regulation by the government can be effective. Lastly, as discussed in the previous chapters, markets do not protect the weak, especially during transitional phases. The state will have to intervene to provide protection, in other words, take care of the welfare of various underprivileged segments of the society. It does not mean that just because there is a need for public goods, regulations, and welfare, the state intervenes heavily in all these areas. We will examine in detail what is the role of the government in each of these areas. Other than these, I want to specifically examine the role of the government in managing the economy.

Public goods

Certain goods and services are required by the society as they add value to the society by increasing efficiency, reducing risk, or providing protection, but no one will want to pay for them as there is no direct ascribable benefit, or the direct ascribable benefit is much lower than the cost of delivering the good or service. Economists call these "public goods". Economists define public goods as non-rivalrous and non-excludable. "Non-rivalrous" means even if a citizen consumes the public good, its quantity will not diminish (or will only diminish very marginally) for others to consume. "Non-exclusionary" means some citizens cannot be excluded from consuming the good or service - either it is available to all or none. Because of this nature, public goods are typically not provided by private entities, as they will not be able to exclude the users/consumers of the public good and charge them for the usage/consumption. A classic example of a public good is the defense of the country. If a country provides a safe and secure environment, everyone enjoys it and no one can be excluded from that. As a result, no one will want to pay directly for safety from external threats, but overall safety is highly desirable by everyone. Other examples of public goods are law enforcement (internal security and contract enforcement), monetary instruments, and infrastructure (roads, water supply, etc.). I will examine the role of the government in each of these.

National defense is one of the legitimate roles of a government. In fact, this is one of the few areas where most liberal economists have an agreement. The size of the defense budget and the scope is where there could be disagreements. All liberals want a minimum defense budget, enough to provide a safe and secure environment within the country. But to provide a safe and secure environment, the government may have to take preventive measures like, for example, targeting terrorists preventively. The problem with preventive self-defense is that it can be misused. This is where a strict self-imposed policy is needed. Along with maintaining defense, at times, military force is also required to help people in other countries. In general, as a rule, liberals support a non-interventionist approach in international matters, but again certain times international responsibilities become inevitable. In these circumstances as well, a clear policy will help mitigate abuse and control defense spending. As can be seen, defense spending can be fraught with subjectivity. As neither am I a defense expert and nor is this a book on defense strategy, I will not comment on the exact scale and scope countries should adopt for their defense forces. Nevertheless, the principles of non-aggression and optimal spending should drive the strategy

Another unambiguous role for the government is law enforcement within the country. This deals with two aspects: internal security (i.e. controlling crime) and enforcing civil contracts. Controlling crime ensures that all entities in an economy stick to the rules. Rule of law is very important for the efficient functioning of markets. Here is where the state will have to play the nightwatchman role. The state has to provide a police force for preventing crime and for delivering justice. It is also very clear that several countries use police force far beyond this role. For example, police are often used for traffic management, which can easily be privatized. Only when there is a crime involved should the police be concerned. The day-to-day management of traffic on roads, monitoring of traffic lights, fining people for violations, etc. can all be done by a private entity. The rights to manage traffic can be auctioned by the local government. The private entity can be funded by the fines collected directly or by the local civic body. A good economist can design an auctioning mechanism that benefits both commuters and the local government. Staunch libertarians argue that police roles can be completely privatized. The positive aspect of the privatization of police is that it can eliminate bureaucratic corruption and inefficiencies. The negative aspect is that privatization can introduce corporate corruption, where the rights of the poor are violated in favor of the rich. As an advocate of minimal government, I agree with the fact that the police force has to be minimal to the extent required for enforcing the law and not beyond. All auxiliary functions can be privatized, including security to certain "important" citizens, traffic management, and protection of private property.

Along with the police, another key piece of law enforcement is the judiciary system. Courts are used for delivering criminal justice and also enforcing civil contracts. Both are very important functions to establish the rule of law and for supporting markets in free operation. Most of the judicial role has to be taken up by the government, especially the criminal justice side. In civil contract enforcement, there could be scenarios where private entities can provide services. Like for example, certain markets use ombudsman to resolve conflicts amongst the participants. In fact, libertarians extend this concept to the extent that there could be private jurisdictions where non-governmental entities can establish jurisdiction. In such a case, entities entering into contracts can freely choose one of the private jurisdictions to enforce the contract. Private jurisdictions are not a new idea but existed in England for several centuries in the form of "Franchise Jurisdictions". Nevertheless, even with the possibility of private jurisdictions, the role of the government remains to a large extent.

Another public good is "infrastructure" - a public good that requires heavy capital investments. These are typically not delivered by markets efficiently either because the investment is very high, they require special rights to deliver infrastructure like the right of way, or the effect on the society is disproportionately higher compared to the revenue that can be earned from the infrastructure. There are arguments for and against the involvement of the government in infrastructure development. The strongest argument in favor of government involvement is that private entities cannot acquire the right of way easily for building long roads, railways, electric lines, etc. For example, imagine a society where all the real estate is held by private entities (individuals or legal persons). Imagine that in that society if a person wants to move goods or services from one part to another he has to negotiate with several property owners for the right of way. This becomes practically impossible on a large scale. Hence, there is some form of centralized planning and intervention required. The logic applies to any kind of infrastructure required for transferring goods or services. Roads and railways for transferring goods and people are one big part of this. Electricity cables, waterways/pipelines, gas/petrol pipelines. etc. are another. Even though there is a need for the state's intervention, the intervention should be limited to establishing a right of way and not beyond. So, for example, it should not be the role of the state to run transportation services on top of roads. The same is the case for railways; the trains running on railroads and routes can be managed privately. Also, this right of way logic does not extend to other forms of transportation; for example, if a private entity can gather enough land it can build a port or an airport. Because both the skies and the waters are not held privately, there is no special right of way required.

Other than the right of way, the reason for government intervention in infrastructure is to provide market access to underserved geographical regions. As the incentive for private entities to build infrastructure in remote or poor parts of a country is less, the government will have to intervene. Here, apart from infrastructure like roads, railways, water lines, electricity, etc., there is also a need for providing infrastructure for services like digital communications, physical space for trading products (like agriculture markets), etc. The idea is to only create a conducive environment for markets to operate in and not to replace the markets.

Another important infrastructure that the government provides across all countries is the monetary system. A monetary system is a special infrastructure that allows citizens to use money, save money, and transfer money. The infrastructure includes central/reserve banks, mints (for minting new money), banking system, and payment/transfer systems. Although most of the downstream activity is privatized, the top-level infrastructure of the monetary system i.e. minting of money and reserve banking is managed by the government. In almost all countries in the world, only a single currency is legal tender. This is the official currency of the country and except in monetary unions (like European monetary union) the supply of this currency is managed by a central authority, typically called the central bank. Central banks, in such cases, have a monopoly on the issue and management of the money. As the banking system is the main channel that the central bank uses to distribute the money, the banking system is highly regulated by the central bank. Although central banks are purported to be independent of the state, they are agents of the state and eventually answerable to the government. As a result, the monetary system is highly monopolized and intervened with by the government. The intervention by the government in the monetary system has significantly increased over the last couple of decades, especially after the popularization of monetary policy as a tool to manage economies by the Ronald Reagan government in the United States and Margaret Thatcher government in the United Kingdom. This role of government has to be cut down in all areas of economic activity. But as long as there is a monopoly of the government on the money, the government will have some role to play in the money supply and monetary system. I will look at some of these issues in the chapter on money.

Regulations

Regulations are a special form of a public good. In the absence of regulations, private entities usually come up with standards or best practices. The difference between standards and regulations is that the flouting of regulations is considered a criminal offense. In cases where two entities enter into a contract (to exchange goods or services) their relationship will be governed by the terms of the contract. If there are no significant asymmetries in power or information, then each party can protect its interests. But in cases where either one party has more information or significantly more economic power than the other party, regulations act as a support. As the weaker party will not be able to fight an expensive legal battle, it will be at a disadvantage. Most of the problems arise when individuals or small corporations become customers of bigger entities. In such cases, there is a case for regulating the market. Most of the protection can come from generic consumer protection laws without too much industry-specific regulation. Where the transactions between the parties can have a very high and irreversible impact, there is a case made by interventionists for additional regulation. Some examples of industries with such transactions are financial services and healthcare. As the financial services industry deals with large amounts of money, any irregularity in transactions in that industry could lead to significant and irrevocable losses to the customer. Similarly, since healthcare deals with the life and limb of customers, any irregularity can impact the customer significantly. I will look at these two industries specifically to highlight the fact that over-regulation has been only detrimental to the consumer. Nevertheless, the claim that such industries should not be regulated at all is also unfounded. We need to critically examine these industries to identify the minimal set of regulations to help the ecosystem and protect the customer. I have specifically chosen these two industries because that is where interventionists forcefully argue for heavy regulation. Apart from such critical industries, specific regulation is also advocated for economic activities that have negative externalities, like impact on the environment. We should examine environmental regulations also to identify the right amount of regulation without impeding economic activity.

Financial services, especially banking services, have been un-regulated for a very long time. Although early forms of regulation were seen in the seventeenth century, fully formalized regulation started with banking acts in various countries. The reasons for regulating financial services are purported to be two-fold: to protect the customer from unforeseen risks and to save the economy from systemic risk emanating from the financial services industry. The risks that a customer is exposed to in the financial services industry are the insolvency of the institution, market risk emanating from market-linked products, and fraud risk in certain cases. All of these three risks are valid risks a customer is exposed to, but what several decades of banking regulation have shown is that regulation does not mitigate the risks. Despite heavy regulation in several countries banks have gone bankrupt wiping away savings of their depositors, investors have lost a significant amount of their investments in financial markets during market meltdowns, and frauds do happen resulting in loss of money of customers. Regulations have nevertheless impeded innovation and competition in the financial services industry. Regulations also have excluded certain customers from buying certain products (like for example complex financial products are not available for retail customers in some countries). This has created disparity by excluding certain customers from the market. Also, smaller businesses are excluded from providing certain services as the regulations increase the cost of carrying the business in this industry, leading to monopolies and inefficient allocation. This is one of the reasons incumbent corporations support regulations. What will help customers, at least in the financial services industry, is better education about products and risks. In a free market, competition ensures that private entities spread more awareness about them. There will be third-party entities that will come up to provide semi regulatory functions like rating of products and services, self-regulation, dispute resolution, etc. Advisors will spring up creating a niche in providing customized advice to customers in choosing the right product. In any case, customers have remedial action against fraud through other laws. Thus there is no strong case for specific regulation of the financial services industry from a customer protection standpoint.

Another reason some people support regulation of the financial services industry is the systemic influence it has on the economy. This is a hangover of the stock market crash of 1929, which has preceded the Great Depression. The argument is that as the financial services industry is the backbone of several other industries it needs to be controlled. The problem with that argument is two-fold. Firstly if the financial services industry is critical it is all the more reason to encourage competition for improving efficiency. Secondly, it has been proven time and again since the Great Depression that regulation has not helped avoid crises in the financial services industry. Some proponents of regulation of banks argue that banks are the primary mechanism through which monetary policy of the government is executed thus they need to be controlled more stringently. As discussed earlier, in fact, excessive government intervention through control of money supply may have caused some of the crises. We will look at this in more detail in the chapter on money.

The only tenable reason for some regulation in the financial services industry is the moral hazard embedded in risk-taking. Banks, being corporations with limited liability, tend to take more risk than is prudent. If the risk reaps positive benefits, they are rewarded and if it reaps losses, the losses are limited by the capital they have deployed. Thus they have a perverse incentive for taking excessive risk. This is a form of what economists call "moral hazard". Moral hazard is more prevalent in individual employees of a company as their downside is limited to losing a job whereas upside can lead to financial benefits in the form of bonuses and career growth. As a result, excessive risk-taking becomes prevalent in industries where risk-taking is easy. This is the case in the financial services industry with many instruments available to take an unbounded risk. Thus, there is a requirement for some amount of supervision, especially in cases where the customer may not fully understand the complex risks involved in the business. Nevertheless, the supervision/regulation need not be on all aspects of the business. A broad overarching approach of risk-based supervision suffices to cover the moral hazard. For example, entities need not be regulated on what kind of products they sell as long as there is no excessive risk being taken.

Healthcare regulation is another controversial area. Here, I am not talking about healthcare provided by the government, which I will discuss as part of the welfare role of the government. The Healthcare industry, especially the drug industry within that is highly regulated in many countries because of the impression that patients need to be protected from both harmful drugs and processes, and also ineffective drugs and processes. Heavy regulation of the healthcare industry eventually increases the cost of administering healthcare to ordinary citizens. There are other industries, the electrical goods industry, for example, that can have a significant impact on the life and limb of their customers yet they are not as heavily regulated. The safety and security of customers are ensured through competition amongst various players. Also, private entities can come up to certify goods as safe to use. These entities, coupled with consumer awareness, can protect the customer from malicious and unsafe practices. This competitive pressure can be established even without dismantling existing regulatory bodies by giving healthcare providers and drug manufacturers the option to opt-out of regulation as long as they communicate the same to their customers. The customers can then choose regulated entities or unregulated entities. Over time, the regulatory bodies will become redundant if citizens start assigning more credibility to other forms of accreditation. What applies to drugs will also apply to other health care services including hospitals, medical devices, diagnostic centers, etc. Even under the current highly regulated environment, there are enough snake oil salesmen in the healthcare industry. A growing market for unproven alternative medicine is proof of that. Like in the case of the financial services industry, customer/patient awareness and minimal, simple regulations is the optimal tool to protect the customer.

Instead of having industry-specific regulation, a generic customer protection framework will work better for society. Customers should be protected from fraud emanating in the form of willful misinformation, concealment of information, breach of contract, and inappropriate selling. Customers in most industries will be protected if these kinds of frauds are criminalized. Existing laws should usually be sufficient to cover these frauds, but if there is a gap, it can be filled using a generic customer protection act. Specific industries can come up with their mechanisms to further protect the customer like accreditation by third parties, self-regulation, and ombudsman for dispute resolution.

Environment and natural resource protection are two of the reasons that can justify some amount of regulation of business. Impact on the environment causes negative externalities, which are not adequately handled in a free market system. Thus there is a need for external intervention. Although common laws against nuisance and trespassing can restrain most harm that could be done to the environment, there are specific cases where the impact is not localized. Examples could be depletion/pollution of ground resources and pollution of air. Activities impacting air specifically have to be regulated as the impact is dissipated not only across the country but also across the globe. As the local impact is less than the global impact, the incentive for local entities to effectively control such activities is less. The same can be said about ocean pollution and, to some extent, river pollution. There are quasi-market solutions to tackle these problems by creating virtual property rights like carbon credits. These have not been hugely effective though. As a result, there is a need for some sort of simple set of standards and rules to regulate the impact.

Welfare

As a principle, liberal economic policies usually do not support welfare policies as they interfere with free markets and also are a burden to the taxpayers. In principle, welfare policies are nothing but forced redistribution of wealth. Having said that, a certain amount of welfare as a safety net is not incompatible with liberal economic policies. To let some people suffer for the sake of upholding market efficiency principles is morally wrong. Apart from having a safety net, welfare also provides stopgap support for people who are looking to change livelihood mechanisms driven by technological or environmental changes. Thus, welfare provided by the government reduces risks for an economy and hence it acts as a public good. At this point, I want to explicitly point out that welfare should be used only as a safety net and not as a way to increase demand in the line of Keynesian stimulus. The level of involvement of the government has to be minimal though. The guiding principles for welfare should be: 1. It should not create distortionary effects on markets, 2. Areas that are absolutely necessary for human sustenance and elimination of suffering should be prioritized. Food, housing, health care, and education typically form this minimal basket of welfare. Other than education, the other areas - housing, food, and health care are absolutely necessary for a decent living. I have added education here, specifically, as education involves a long gestational investment with multi-generational impact.

The problem with providing specific services for free is that it interferes with market-clearing mechanisms and provides perverse incentives. For example, free housing can cause citizens to take up houses that they don't like in locations that may not be suitable for them to earn money. Similarly, free food obstructs the freedom to choose for citizens. A better alternative to providing free food, health care, and housing is to provide a basic income that can act as a safety net for citizens. The income can be used for buying health insurance, food, and renting houses from the market. Part of the income can also be used to upgrade skills to be able to get a better paying job. The citizen herself can do the right allocation. Not only will this help increase the market participation of the poor as well, but this will also reduce implementation costs for welfare schemes. Such an income guarantee scheme or universal basic income scheme has been supported by free-market proponents like Hayek and Friedman as well. I will look into the details of such schemes and the advantage they might incur to the society in the chapter on universal basic income.

The premise for universal basic income is that all other subsidies and free schemes should be subsumed by this scheme. Specifically, schemes that incentivize people to work in a certain industry, for example, seed and fertilizer subsidies for farmers or subsidies for small-scale industries, should be eliminated. Such incentives make sure that the citizens involved in them remain poor without being able to explore more attractive alternatives to employment. Unconditional transfer of money to everyone is a better mechanism than incentives for specific activities, or subsidization of certain services, or for that matter any other interventionist measures. Having said that, we will specifically evaluate healthcare and education interventions. The reason being, both of these services do not have instantaneous costs and benefits. In the case of healthcare, the costs will be contingent on certain events and may not be predictable in advance. In the case of education, the costs will be today and the benefits in the future. Market mechanisms might fail in such cases where full information is not present with the decision maker at the time of making the decision.

Healthcare requires a special mention because, unlike other welfare requirements, healthcare requirements are not homogenous. Every individual will have a unique healthcare requirement. Even for a single individual, the requirement varies quite a bit over time. Thus, it cannot be easily covered by universal income. There are several ways that policymakers are addressing the problem of providing healthcare. They fall into three categories: 1. State providing healthcare services, 2. State paying (partly or wholly) for healthcare charges of private entities, 3. State paying (partly or wholly) for insurance, which will cover healthcare costs. In the second option, the state is becoming an insurance company. The last option is either implemented as the state identifying an insurer and paying it directly or the state paying tokens/money to citizens who can choose their own insurer. Each of these has different issues. The first option, i.e. the state delivering healthcare, eventually leads to inefficiencies because of lack of competition. This makes the queues longer and the quality of service poorer. Innovations will also be subdued. The second option, which is equivalent to the state becoming an insurance company, also has a similar problem although to a smaller extent as the inefficiency will only be in insurance administration and not in the whole healthcare chain. Another problem that could arise is that only hospitals with lower quality of service might register to provide healthcare if the government fixes the payment terms. A third issue is the moral hazard of hospitals inflating bills by prescribing unwarranted procedures. The third option of the state sponsoring insurance is a better option than the other two, especially if the citizen is given the option to choose the insurance company as this brings back the competitive forces to healthcare welfare. Insurance companies can compete with each other on their coverage of hospitals, pricing, and quality of service. Citizens can choose from any insurance plan that suits their needs the best. The only bone of contention is that several citizens may not have enough information and understanding to choose the right plan.

I must add that, only because of the extremely low level of awareness with regards to healthcare and health insurance and also because even well aware citizens wrongly estimate the probability of the need for healthcare, the state may have to intervene. Again, like in the case of financial services, advisors and information dissemination platforms can help. In fact, if citizens have enough understanding of health insurance and the need for it, there need not be separate schemes for healthcare and it can be covered as a part of universal basic income. If there is a concern that universal basic income will be misused, then providing tokens that can be used specifically for healthcare is a good alternative.

Education is another important aspect of welfare. There are specific reasons why education should be treated differently as opposed to other forms of welfare. School education has a long gestation in yielding financial returns, so parents may not be willing to voluntarily spend on schooling for their kids. Apart from this, having every member of the society educated can have a significant impact on society itself, this is a positive externality of education. Because of these aspects of education, the price of education may not truly reflect both the actual value and the value perceived by citizens. So, most citizens, if asked to pay a high amount for education, may not be willing to educate their children. Many governments solve this problem by providing education for free, directly through public schools. As a result, not only are schools run inefficiently, but the government also decides what should be taught and how. This takes away the freedom of choice. A much better alternative is for the state to provide for kids vouchers to be used for preferred private schools. With a voucher system, the government still controls what constitutes a school education albeit with some freedom of choice given to the citizen. The controls and regulations are not completely avoided but significantly reduced. It goes without mention that higher education and vocational training, which can yield immediate financial fruits, need not be regulated or subsidized in any way.

Economic management

Economists of the twentieth century have also built a fourth role for the government - management of the economy. This started with the Great Depression. Economists argued that the Great Depression illustrated the need for government intervention to fight economic shocks. Governments intervene in the economy mainly through fiscal policy and monetary policy.

Fiscal policy is the main tool that was tried at the time of the Great Depression to fight economic slowdown. Fiscal policy as a tool to manage the economy was introduced by Lord Keynes as a medicine to counter the so-called slowdown in demand[4]. Keynesians (i.e. followers of Keynes) claim that total demand for goods and services (called Aggregate Demand by economists) in an economy may be at times lower than the supply (called Aggregate Supply by economists) and government intervention is needed to correct this. In an economy, Aggregate Demand (AD) is given by

---

[4] Keynes, J. M. (1936). *The general theory of employment, interest and money.* New York City: Harcourt, Brace.

Aggregate Demand (AD)

=

Private Consumption (C) + Private Investment (I) + Government
Spending (G)

Where Private Consumption (C) and Private Investment (I) include
consumption and investment by both individuals and companies. Keynesians
argue that if C and I drop for some reason, because of some shock, the
government needs to step in to increase AD by increasing Government
Spending. On the other hand, if C and I increase and the economy heats up,
Keynesians argue that the government needs to decrease its spending to
reduce AD. This logic has remained the bedrock for Keynesian economics for
a long time from the 1930s to 1970s. Vestiges of this logic remain in
policymaking and economic thought process. But not all economic schools of
thought support this argument. The monetary school argues that there is no
need for the government to intervene in the economy through increasing or
reducing its spending. To maintain economic stability, they argue, the money
supply needs to be regulated by the government or its agency. This is known
as monetary policy.

Classical liberal economics rejects the effectiveness of both fiscal policy and
monetary policy. Concerning fiscal policy, liberal economists argue that the
government cannot create goods and services by itself, and hence, just by
spending more, they will not be able to increase productivity efficiently.
Markets, left to themselves, will adjust so that there will not be any excess
demand or supply at an aggregate level. This is known as Walras's law after the
famous nineteenth-century French economics Léon Walras. If there is a drop
in Aggregate Demand then the prices of goods and services will automatically
adjust to a level where the Aggregate Demand meets the Aggregate Supply. For
this to happen all markets, i.e. goods, services, labor, and capital markets,
should operate freely. If the markets operate freely, the prices and quantities
will correct quickly to absorb any shock thus obviating the need for an
inefficient solution in the form of government intervention.

With regards to monetary policy, classical economists believe that money
supply only affects nominal values and does not have any long term impact
on real values like inflation-adjusted GDP or total real wealth of citizens. In
the short term, monetary policy can have a distortionary effect. Monetary
policy takes away the freedom of money markets. I will look at this more in
detail in the chapter on money. The gist of liberal economics is that the
government has little role to play in economic management either through
monetary policy or fiscal policy.

To sum up...

Currently, governments across the world regulate business activities too much and spend too much on welfare and other activities. A lot of this can be cut down leading to a state where the state is taking just the role of a nightwatchman providing security and safety. The basic public goods that should be managed by the state include national security, law, and order. Infrastructure can be partly developed by the state where there is a right of way involved that cannot be obtained by private entities or in cases where, because of geographic reasons, private infrastructure development does not become viable. The state does not need to regulate most industries, including the financial services industry. Where regulation is necessary, i.e. in industries with highly complex products having a significant impact on customers like pharmaceuticals and healthcare industries, the regulation should be simple. Rather than having a fixed regime, entities should have an option to choose from various private certification schemes. This ensures that information asymmetry between customers and companies is reduced at the same time excessive government control is avoided. Governments also need to cut down on most of the specific subsidies to industries and individuals. All the welfare schemes of the government should be replaced by universal basic income schemes coupled with vouchers for specific needs of health insurance and education.

The minimal government ensures that markets are free to operate and allocate most efficiently. Each individual can have more liberty to choose the kind of life she wants to lead. In addition to this, the minimal government also means taxation in the economy can be low, thus leading to more prosperity in the hands of citizens. I will look at what kind of taxation would be ideal to support liberty and ensure prosperity in the next chapter.

Chapter 5

On taxation

Taxes are an evil - a necessary evil, but still an evil, and the fewer we have of them the better.[1]

- Winston Churchill

The same guiding principles of natural justice and allocative efficiency that I have applied to derive free-market principles in the chapter on economic liberty can be extended to derive ideal or close to ideal taxation. Even though libertarians consider all taxation as evil, as it disincentivizes production, taxation itself is unavoidable and some types of taxes are better than the others. I will examine various types of taxation in this chapter. Some of them are already popular, some not in use, and some are used sparingly by governments. Some economists argue for a single tax system where only one type of tax is charged and some argue for a multiple tax system. We will look at specifically:

1. Personal income tax,

2. Land tax,

3. Corporate income tax,

4. Wealth tax,

5. Consumption tax,

6. Severance and Pigouvian taxes, and

7. Tax on monetary transactions.

Irrespective of the type of tax system, it goes without saying that it has to be simple and the overall taxation has to be low.

---

[1] House of Commons Debate 12 February 1907 vol 169 cc58-152. Retrieved from: https://api.parliament.uk/historic-hansard/commons/1907/feb/12/kings-speech-motion-for-an-address

Personal income tax

John Locke, a 17th-century English philosopher who is considered the father of liberalism, while setting out the principles of liberty said "Everyman has a property in his person; this nobody has a right to but himself. The labor of his body and the work of his hand, we may say, are properly his."[2] Property rights are considered a key aspect of economic liberty. The exact definition of property varies from one proponent of liberty to another. But most agree that a person's body and whatever is produced using the labor of the body should belong to only that person. Nobody else can lay a claim on this. This should be the guiding principle for liberal economic policies including policies on taxation. Some argue that the logic should be extended to property owned in the form of land and natural resources. Others argue that any improvements done on land belong to the person making the improvement unequivocally, but the land itself belongs to the society. This particular thought process elaborated by Henry George in the late nineteenth century is called Georgism. Georgism not only derives its principles from the principle of natural justice but also to achieve allocative efficiency. Henry George argued that any taxation on labor is counterproductive as it disincentivizes people from working harder (however small the disincentive might be)[3].

If you keep aside the definition of property, it is very clear that any tax on income from labor is a disincentive to earn more. In other words, the fruits of labor should belong to the person toiling for them and it should not be redistributed to others. To elaborate on the point, let us start with a simple case, where I share the household workload with my partner. I do the dishes and my partner cooks. As we are doing a simple division of labor, there is no need for either one of us to pay taxes. Now let us extend this example, let us say I fix my neighbor's computer and in lieu, he fixes my furniture. In this case, as it is informal labor exchange many people feel that there should be no taxes involved, although in a strict sense barter is covered under taxation laws in most countries. Let us extend it further, I fix my neighbor's computer and he promises to do one hour of my work in the future, to remember the promise he gives a coupon. Most people will say this transaction is also not taxable. But instead of giving coupons if he gives me money, suddenly, most people and definitely all governments agree that the transaction should be taxed in some form or another. The government gets involved even though all

---

[2] Locke, J. (2004). *Second Treatise of Government*. United States: Barnes & Noble Books. Page 17.

[3] George, H. (1973). *Progress and poverty; an inquiry into the cause of industrial depressions and of increase of want with increase of wealth: The remedy*. New York City: AMS Press.

we have done is just to systematize the concept of division of labor and made it easy using money. If I can produce all goods and services that I need on my own, then there is no taxation, but if we as a society use division of labor to achieve the same end more efficiently, the government takes a piece of that pie. This is contradictory to the principles of economics: the more efficient the society tries to be, the more taxes there will be.

So why then personal taxation still exists with so much prevalence? Governments and economists justify personal tax using two arguments: 1. It helps in the distribution of wealth, 2. The personal income arises partly because of the ecosystem developed by society; hence part of the income has to be shared with the society. The income distribution argument looks valid at a superficial level. But it does not hold ground upon deeper analysis. That is because any income that is not taxed will remain with the person earning the income as wealth. The wealth of each person is typically invested back in the economy through consumption or as the capital of a business. Thus even without taxation, wealth redistribution already happens in society through consumption. Even the money that is invested by the savers will eventually go back into the economy. Governments and economists who favor taxation as a tool to redistribute wealth argue that taxation is a direct way to take money from the rich to support the poor. But this argument does not hold ground as even the middle class is taxed in most economies and they are the ones who get affected the most by the taxation. Thus, taxation is a very inefficient form of redistribution of wealth. In fact, the main reason governments actually have taxation is to support large government spending. Once a government gets used to a level of spending, it is very tough to roll it back. Taxing personal income is a way to support this high spending.

The second argument for taxing personal income is that society contributes to the income of a person by providing the ecosystem and infrastructure. But it can be argued that individuals have been providing services for millennia even before the society got organized formally. There is no denying the fact that humans use infrastructure developed by the society/government to deliver services. For example, we use telephone networks or roads to provide our services to others in society. A better way to charge individuals for using the ecosystem/infrastructure is to directly charge the usage rather than through taxing the income. Other than incentivizing individuals to be more productive, this also ensures better allocative efficiency.

Another big argument for exempting personal taxes is that in today's connected world, it is easy to provide service from any location. This is especially true for certain types of services. In the current times, where many services can be delivered from any part of the world, these services will gravitate to countries with zero tax regimes. Thus, in the interest of retaining a high-quality workforce, taxes must be kept at zero. Removing personal income taxes makes the tax code very simple, eliminating a large part of the tax administration bureaucracy. There will be no need to monitor the transactions of individuals. Individuals can freely move their wealth across various assets (including assets outside the country) without any scrutiny or compliance requirements. This can increase the liberty of individuals to a large extent.

As discussed in the previous chapters, the arguments used for the abrogation of personal income tax may not be directly extended to corporations. Similarly, all personal income should not qualify for zero taxation. For example, income obtained in place of profits from a corporation, like bonuses, etc., cannot be attributed purely to labor. Hence, such income may not be exempted from tax. As it could be tough to determine which part of income comes from labor and which part comes from profits of a business, an easier way out is to put a constant tax on income above a certain level (the level has to be kept very high though). Also, income obtained from land or other natural resources need not be automatically exempt; I will look at these aspects in the sections on land and severance taxes. Having said that, a broad range of activities can be exempted from taxation, including speculative activities, activities involving intellectual capabilities, physical capabilities, or specific skills. It does not matter if the income is earned in the form of wages or some other form (selling goods and services, trading, etc.) We will look at specific cases of income from corporations and income from the land in subsequent sections, as these have to be treated differently.

There are very few countries that have zero personal tax regimes. Most of the countries with zero tax regimes are either oil-rich countries with significant sources of income from natural resources or island nations looking to attract investors by being tax havens. Most countries in the world have some sort of progressive taxation. Progressive taxation is a system where the proportion of tax to the income keeps increasing as the income keeps increasing. There will be an income level below which there is no tax. But as income increases beyond this level, the tax rate (as a percentage of income) keeps going up. Sometimes, some deductions are allowed from the income before tax is calculated (like for example medical expenses). The tax rate that is applied for a certain slab of income is called the marginal tax rate. The highest marginal tax rates for various countries in the world can go from 0% to as high as 60% or more. Even some of the richer western countries have significantly high marginal tax rates to fund their welfare schemes. Taxation enables the government to expand its roles and once a government has acquired power, it is very unlikely that it will give up that power. Hence, taxes, in general, tend to only go up unless there is a drastic reform. Completely eliminating personal income taxes could be one such drastic reform.

Tax on land

I have briefly touched upon how land is different from other assets. Man does not produce the land. It has been acquired historically through homesteading principle (i.e. gaining rights on land through original appropriation) or through violent means (i.e. wars and occupations). Thus, land inherently belongs to society. Does that mean all land should be nationalized? I don't think so. If only the government has rights over land and it makes all the decisions on how the land should be used, it will be inefficiently allocated, as it does not respond to the market prices. Thus having private land can help in the efficient use of land. Also, current owners of the land have bought the land with their fruits of labor. Thus it is unjust to take away the land the people own currently. There isn't much to be gained by questioning the historic basis of the allocation of rights on the land. Nevertheless, to make land usage efficient, a tax on land owned can be introduced. In most countries, such tax already exists in the form of property tax, but the level of this taxation is minuscule compared to other forms of tax at the moment. There are multiple reasons for imposing a tax on land. In fact, Henry George argued that land tax is the only tax that should be imposed[4]. Any other form of tax will typically end up penalizing consumption or production. Whereas, land tax will only penalize the owner if the land is not being used efficiently. Some libertarians are against this argument as they support the absolute rights of property. I do not agree with them because land is unlike any other property. The justification for this hinges principally upon four arguments: 1. Landholding can lead to the creation of monopolies, 2. Tax on land ensures optimal usage of the land, 3. The value of land hinges upon development of the neighborhood, and lastly, 4. Tax on land corrects inequity established historically. We will look at each of these aspects in detail.

Monopolies are created because a particular entity owns rights over a property and those rights create barriers for other entities to compete. The properties that can create monopolies can be a wide variety including intellectual property, brand, customer data, land, or access to natural resources. Humans create most of the other properties like intellectual property or brand. Thus even if their ownership creates a monopoly, there is reason to not tax them. Only unfair practices related to the monopoly can be regulated. But when it comes to land and natural resources, any monopolization is naturally unfair, as humans do not create the land itself. Although the improvements on land can be completely exempt from this line

---

[4] Ibid.

of argument. Thus taxing land can be a justified means to penalize the monopolization of land and associated natural resources.

The next point, which is closely related to the argument regarding monopolization, is that at certain times, land may not be effectively used. This can be seen in cases where a real estate developer hoards on to land and does not develop the properties in anticipation of a speculative gain. This can lock up land and cause an inefficient allocation. The prices of land and related assets can shoot up without benefiting the economy. This hoarding can be discouraged by taxing holding of land irrespective of whether it generates income or not. This will ensure large parcels of idle land to be utilized giving a big boost to economic productivity. The value of the land itself could drop as buyers of land will capitalize the present value of future tax payments, and a drop in the value of land is a good eventuality for citizens and businesses. Reduction in the price of land in dollar terms does not reduce the productivity of the land or total supply of the land. Reduction in the value of land can provide an opportunity for businesses and citizens to buy land and use it productively. There could be a sudden drop in the wealth of landowners at the time of introduction of such a tax, to compensate for that landowners can be given a one-time tax credit.

Another argument that strongly supports taxing landholding is that a big portion of the value of land comes from the development of the neighborhood. A well-developed society and economic ecosystem pull the value of the land up significantly. Logically, the landholder has to pay back to society for this. The collected taxes can be used for further improvement of the neighborhood. For example, an addition of a park or a police station could add further value to the property itself.

The last point comes from reasoning that most of the land has been acquired in the past through violent means, i.e. through occupation. This has also created a significant wealth disparity that persisted for ages. I'm not advocating a Marxist solution of socialization of land, as that would create more chaos and violence. Current owners of the land are not the ones to have caused the violence of the past. Nevertheless, if there were no private appropriation of land originally, there would not be any owners of land today. Instead of making land public, a good way to correct historic injustice is to tax the landholders.

Having established that land taxes are justified and necessary for efficient economic operations, we need to examine two critical aspects: how much to tax and how to tax land? I am not going into the exact level of tax that should be charged, as that would depend on specific local requirements and circumstances. There are several arguments on how much to tax. The simplest approach would be to make the tax a percentage of the value of the land. The percentage can be fixed based on the fiscal state of the government, i.e. what is the total expenditure of the government. If the land tax can cover all the basic expenses of the government (as discussed in the previous chapter including welfare) then there is no need for introducing any other tax. Another approach could be charging tax as a percentage on shadow rental income (i.e. rental income if the land is rented out at market rates).

As land will be valuable to any owner be it an individual or a corporate entity, the land tax should be charged to individuals or corporate entities without discrimination. As most of the land's value comes from the neighborhood, local authorities should be the ones charging land tax. Either municipalities or county/state governments will be in the ideal position to charge the tax. As their income is linked to the value of the land they will take all measures to increase the usage of land available, including attracting industry and increasing the productivity of the land. Part of the land tax revenue can be shared with the national government for improving national infrastructure.

Corporate tax

One of the principles I have been stressing on quite a bit is that corporate entities cannot be treated in the same vein as natural persons (individuals). I will look at how corporate entities differ from individuals. Limited liability is a unique right that corporate entities enjoy that is not available to individuals. This right ensures that the maximum losses the shareholders can incur are the investment that they have made. Even if a corporate entity has a bigger liability, the shareholders cannot be forced to pay up more money. If the corporation makes high profits, the profits are distributed to the shareholders, whereas if it makes significant losses, the corporation will simply declare bankruptcy rather than take more money from the shareholders. Because of this asymmetric payoff, corporate entities are incentivized to take more risks. The term "corporate entity" includes several different legal structures where shareholders and the management are segregated, and there is limited liability for the shareholders. These structures include public corporations, private corporations, limited liability partnerships, etc.

Another big aspect of liability is the liability arising out of criminal offenses. Unlike natural persons, corporate entities cannot be imprisoned[5]. Fines are the usual way to punish corporations for the wrongs they do. Fines do not create the guilt, shame, and repentance that punishments create in

---

[5] In some cases, the management of the corporate entity can be imprisoned for criminal offenses, but most corporate offenses are punished through fines.

individuals. Thus, even crime can become an economic decision rather than a moral decision for corporations. This further incentivizes the corporations to take more risks. The risk taken by corporations affects the shareholders and also the rest of the society, as this risk has a bearing on employees, customers, and suppliers of the corporate entity.

Another right that corporations have is the right to hold a property for as long as they are going concern (i.e. they can pay off their liabilities). Thus, corporate entities can hold on to properties for several generations. These properties can be in the form of intellectual property, brand, customer data, physical assets, etc. Most of the value corporations generate is because of these properties. Once the corporations own the property, subsequent profits are in a way rent from the property. Individuals have a variation of this right in the form of inheritance, but it cannot be as efficiently executed as in the case of corporations. The right to hold property by non-natural entities is a right bestowed upon them by the legal system.

In return for these rights, a corporate entity needs to pay back to society. A natural repercussion of this principle is that the tax freedom we have discussed with regards to personal income tax does not apply to corporations. As they enjoy limited liability and other rights, they need to pay compensation for those rights bestowed upon them by society. Thus, corporate tax is a justifiable tax. In a way, corporate tax is a licensing fee for utilizing the protections offered by the jurisdiction of the country. If corporate tax is seen as a fee and not as a way to redistribute wealth, then it logically follows that the tax should be lower than the current prevalent rates. Current corporate tax rates range anywhere from 0% to more than 60% (when indirect taxes and dividend distribution taxes are also taken into account)[6]. Median corporate tax across countries is around 30%, excluding dividend distribution tax. Apart from high corporate tax in various countries, there are additional taxes in the form of dividend taxes, value-added taxes, etc. Instead of having a range of taxes being imposed on a company, a small tax on the net income (profit) of the company should be enough as a compensation to the legal jurisdiction provided to the companies. The exact amount of tax could change from country to country though.

As the rights given to a corporate entity are applicable throughout a country, the taxation should also be done at a national level, unlike the land tax. This tax can be utilized to provide better business infrastructure, like for example

---

[6] Ortiz-Ospina, E. (2016). *Taxation*. OurWorldinData.org [Web]. Retrieved from: https://ourworldindata.org/taxation.

infrastructure for solving customer grievances. If the role of government is kept to the minimum, there is no need for high corporate taxes. Like in the case of land taxes, I'm not getting into the exact level of tax that needs to be charged as that depends on the status of the economy, among other things.

In certain cases, executives of corporate entities take a significant amount of bonuses and salaries, which are indirectly linked to the profits of the company. These should be treated as profit distribution rather than labor charges. This logic justifies charging a tax on personal income beyond a certain threshold, especially for key employees of a company. This is to ensure that personal tax freedom is not exploited to avoid corporate tax. It goes without saying that the threshold for such taxation should be very high. Another point to keep in mind is that quasi corporations like trusts, proprietorship firms, or partnerships, which act, as pass-through vehicles can be exempt from corporate taxes. This is to ensure that there are legal ways to come together and do business without taking full advantage of the limited liability rights of corporate entities.

Wealth tax

Wealth tax is very closely related to personal tax. Wealth is nothing but accumulated income over time. Thus the logic applied to personal tax should apply to wealth tax as well. In an income tax regime, where personal tax is zero if a citizen consumes all the income and does not save anything, she is not charged any tax. If another citizen saves part of the income, to use the income in the future, she should also not be taxed any amount as it is just a preference of time of consumption that the citizen is exercising. The accumulated savings are nothing but the wealth of the citizens. Thus it logically follows that if personal tax is eliminated, wealth tax should also be eliminated. The only justification for wealth tax is for achieving direct wealth redistribution. This is more of a socialistic objective and not related to funding of the government. Some might argue that a small wealth tax will not hurt the rich but could save the poor. That is not exactly true as the wealth accumulated by the rich is usually invested back in the economy and will eventually benefit everyone. Adding a government layer will only make the process less efficient. In any case, most of the wealth is stored as land or holdings in companies. As there can be a tax on both of them, an additional wealth tax will tantamount to double taxation.

A special type of wealth not created by the citizen is inheritance. Libertarians are split on this topic, to say the least. Some argue that children do not have an automatic right to inherit, as they have not earned the property through labor. Some, on the other hand, argue that interference in the form of transfer of property after death should be treated in the same lines as consumption or gifting during the lifetime i.e. the liberties accorded to a person during a lifetime need not end after death. From the perspective of economics, wealth for progeny is one of the motivations for earning income and contributing to the economy in the process. This argument supports not taxing inheritance. Another argument against inheritance tax is that the wealth accumulation is anyways covered by other taxes like property and corporate income taxes, leading to double taxation. Having said that, like the corporate structure I have discussed earlier, inheritance is a concept created and protected by the laws of society. Inheritance or gifting in general transfers rights of certain properties. This transfer of rights is protected by the legal system of the country. So as compensation for that protection, a small amount can be parted as tax. Thus there is a justification for a small inheritance tax, equivalent to legal fee.

Capital gains tax

Some countries impose capital gains tax - a tax on income earned through the selling of assets at a price above their purchase price. Capital gains can be achieved from the sale of assets like shares in companies, real estate, and even bonds. Capital gains occur because of two reasons: 1. The underlying asset has become more valuable as it is generating more income. 2. The investor identifies an undervalued asset and sells when the value has increased. If the capital gains accrue because of the income of the underlying asset then tax on those gains amounts to double taxation as underlying income in companies is anyways taxed, if the asset is real estate then the land is already taxed. If the capital gains accrue because of the skill of the investor, then again I argue that there is no need to tax the gains if the investor is an individual, as any income generated because of the skill of a person should not be taxed. Any capital gains accrued by a company will be the business income of the company and can be taxed as part of the corporate income tax. Eliminating capital gains tax and treating it like any other income, where individuals are not taxed and corporate entities are taxed at a small rate, will also reduce barriers in capital markets. This can make capital markets more efficient, where decisions are made purely on economic merit and not because of tax laws.

Tax on consumption

Tax on consumption, variously called value-added tax (VAT) or goods and services tax (GST) has become a popular method for taxing consumers. Going by different names, these taxes are charged on the value of goods or services sold. I call it a tax on consumption because the result is that the tax is loaded onto the total amount of consumption of goods and services. The proponents of a consumption tax argue that it is easier to administer, as most goods and services leave a digital trail of the transaction.

There are several problems with a consumption-based tax system though. The first problem with consumption-based taxation is that it is regressive in nature. Regressive taxation is a system in which the poor are taxed more as a percentage of their income or wealth than the rich. This is because the poor in an economy tend to consume more and save less (in proportion to their income), thus a consumption tax can lead to a higher percentage of their income going towards taxes. This is contrary to social justice.

Another problem with consumption-based taxes relates to the tax credit system. To avoid double counting, usually, if a business sells some goods or services and charges a VAT/GST to its customers and it also pays consumption tax on the inputs used for the good or service, then only the net tax needs to be paid to the government. In other words, the business gets tax credits for the tax paid on goods or services it consumes. Larger businesses can take advantage of this to reduce their overall tax liability, but small businesses may not be able to take advantage of this, as they may not be paying consumption tax on all the goods or services they consume, especially if they buy from the informal/non-taxable sector or if a major part of their input is their personal labor. Thus, again the smaller businesses tend to pay more tax as a proportion to their profits.

There is one more issue with VAT with input credit - it is not too different from income tax, and hence it is superfluous. What is consumption for one person is income for another person. Thus consumption tax is just the other side of the same coin as income tax. For example, if a person takes the services of a plumber and gets charged a service tax it is equivalent to charging the plumber tax on income. It is just a mechanical fact whether the tax is charged on top of the service or it is deducted from the service fee. This same simplistic case can be extended to even a complex transaction. Thus, taxing consumption need not be economically far superior compared to income tax. In a perfect world, if all the outputs and all the inputs of business are charged at the same consumption tax rate, then, in effect, business is getting charged a fixed percentage on the difference of the value of output and input. In other words, the business is getting charged a percentage of the profits it makes. Let us take an example in an economy with 10% VAT rate, where a business sells goods for $110, which includes a VAT of $10. The business uses an input material of $88, which includes a VAT of $8. The business gets a credit of $8 as it has paid the VAT as part of input cost. The net profit of the business will be $20 as illustrated by the calculations in Table 5.1.

Table 5.1. Calculation Example of VAT with Credit

The sale price of goods	$100	....	a
VAT on the sale price of goods	$10	....	b=10% of a
Total Cost to the customer	$110	....	c=a+b
Cost of input (without VAT)	$80	....	d
VAT on input	$8	....	e=10% of d
Cost of input with VAT	$88	....	f=d+e
Input VAT credit	$8	....	g=e
The total VAT payable to the government	$2	....	h=b-g
Net profit after VAT	$20	....	j=c-i-h

The income of the business without taxes is $22 and after paying the VAT it is $20, as the government collects $2 as VAT. The same objective can be achieved by charging 9.09% of income tax on $22 of income (9.09% is 1-1/(1+10%)). Charging a flat VAT rate of r with input credit is equivalent to charging an income tax of 1-1/(1+r). I accept that this is a simplistic example and in the real world, it could be a lot more complex because of differences in the consumption tax rate for various categories of goods and services. Also, businesses use various accounting methodologies to calculate income, which can create different outflows of income tax vis-à-vis an equivalent VAT. For example, capital expenditure is depreciated over time while calculating income for the purpose of income tax, whereas the input credit on capital expenditure is typically taken in a single year while calculating VAT payable. Nevertheless, this example illustrates the broad equivalence of income tax and consumption tax, hence making one of these taxes redundant. So, there is no point in having value-added taxation in addition to an income tax other than to complicate matters and putting smaller businesses at a disadvantage. As per our arguments on personal income tax, for goods and services provided by individuals (unlike private limited companies), consumption tax or value-added tax should not be charged. For corporations, it does not matter whether consumption tax is charged or income tax is charged. In some cases, one of them might be better than the other because of operational issues or legacy issues. In any case, only one of the two should remain. This can significantly reduce the complexity of the tax system.

Severance and Pigouvian taxes

As I have stressed in earlier chapters, the environment and natural resources belong to society. But most economic activities directly or indirectly leave a footprint on the environment and also consume natural resources. Society has to be compensated for this through taxes on the use of natural resources and the creation of externalities that affect the environment. The first of these taxes is called severance tax and the second is called Pigouvian tax. The severance tax is named so because it is charged at the time a natural resource, for example, petroleum, is extracted, i.e. severed, for economic use. This tax can be charged on a variety of natural resources including coal, water, soil/sand, petroleum/natural gas, etc. This tax is in addition to the tax on owning land resources. Part of the severance tax, especially if it is charged on the extraction of petroleum and other non-renewable natural resources, could be kept as a reserve for the development of renewable sources of energy in the future. An extended case of a severance tax is the government nationalizing all natural resources and selling the output to generate revenues. Although this is not seen as taxation it is in a way taxing the society through the extraction of natural resources. Oil-rich countries have adopted this policy. This can ease the burden on other economic activities as they can be exempt from taxes. The problem with this approach is that the natural resources may not be efficiently used if pricing and production decisions are taken by a monopoly (i.e. the government), nevertheless, it is socially justifiable as natural resources belong to the overall society.

Pigouvian tax, named after the economist Arthur Cecil Pigou, is a tax on activities causing negative externalities like pollution. This tax is mainly imposed to collect from the causes of the externality an amount that is equivalent to the negative effect. Thus, the true cost of economic activity is taken into consideration while making decisions. Pigouvian tax can be used as a revenue source to fund activities that control pollution. For example, revenue from the Pigouvian tax can be used to clean rivers, plant trees, etc. The problem with Pigouvian tax is that pollution by a particular activity is tough to measure and monitor. Technology can aid in measuring carbon emissions but still, it will involve a large setup to measure pollution across various economic activities. An easier way to tax pollution is to tax consumption of carbon-emitting energy sources like oil, gas, coal, wood. This can be a special form of consumption tax. The right amount of tax can be computed based on the cost to society of the emissions. This will require a detailed scientific and economic analysis, which is beyond the purview of this book. The tax once charged at the time of consumption will automatically get priced into all the downstream services. For example, tax on coal will be factored into thermal electricity price and tax on jet fuel consumption will creep into prices of airline tickets. All economic decisions to use any fossil fuels directly or indirectly, will eventually factor in the environmental cost of that decision.

An alternative to a tax on pollution (also called carbon tax as most emissions consist of carbon dioxide) is a framework where carbon emission is capped and the rights to emit are traded in the market. This can bring in market price discovery. A carbon tax fixes the price of emission and allows the amount of emissions to vary whereas a carbon emission trading framework caps the amount of emissions but allows the cost of emission to vary. Both systems have their advantages and disadvantages and economic thought is still work in progress as to what is the best way to internalize the environmental externalities of business.

Tax on monetary transactions

A not so orthodox method of generating revenue for the government is to put a fee on using monetary services. For example, a government can deduct a small amount from every monetary transaction, including payments and bank transfers. As I will discuss in the next chapter, money currently is a monopoly of the government. The government can take advantage of this to fund its other expenses. This is the remuneration the government gets for setting up and managing the monetary institution. As the amount of money transferred across the economy (also called velocity of money) is very high compared to the income of companies or individuals, even a small tax could suffice to contribute a big amount of revenue. As we will see in the next chapter, money is nothing but an entry in a ledger of the central bank, so collecting fees on transactions is quite straightforward for the central bank to implement. Since the central government is responsible for managing the monetary infrastructure, the tax collection should also go to the central government.

There is a caveat here though. I assumed that tax on monetary transactions is justified because of the service being provided by the government. This is true, but people have accepted government monetary services only because governments have banned all other monetary instruments other than currencies issued by them to be used as legal tender. Thus, inherently establishing a monopoly. Any fee on this service is an exploitation of this monopoly. As I will argue in the next chapter, this is the biggest monopoly that governments across the world have established and it has to be eliminated for the full development of the free market. Once other forms of currency are established the government can still charge a fee for monetary transactions on government-issued money, but then citizens will have a choice to choose the monetary instruments/system most suitable to them.

To sum up, minimal taxation ensures that citizens are free to indulge in the profession of their choice. Having a single primary tax source, preferably tax on land supported by smaller auxiliary taxes like severance and Piguovian taxes and a moderate corporate tax, can stimulate economic activities significantly. This framework reduces the monetary burden and also the overhead of compliance and paperwork. This can give citizens back the liberty of profession without penalizing them for productive activities and in turn, can increase prosperity for all.

Chapter 6

On money

Could money be made of paper at pleasure, every sovereign in Europe would be as rich as he pleased. But the truth is, that it is a bubble and the attempt vanity.[1]

- Thomas Paine

Money is the lubricant that drives the economy. No book on economics is complete without a discussion about money, the role it plays, and how it can be used to better achieve economic objectives. Although we use the term money on a daily basis, the concept of money is much more complex than it looks on the face of it and the history of money is fascinating in itself. Before the introduction of paper money, for a long time, gold was used as money. Gold acts as a medium of exchange and also as a store of value. As long as gold coins were used as a tool for exchanging value, the power of a government on the supply of money is limited. Gold, any metal for that matter, has its own limitations - mainly it is tough to carry around. Thus arose the need for paper money. Although paper money was used in China for a long time, it was introduced in the form of banknotes around the middle of the 17th century in Europe. As these notes were issued by private entities and were linked to gold coins, the government still had limited control over them. As governments tried to establish more control over money, they regulated the issuance of such notes. These regulations eventually led to the banning of all forms of tender other than those issued by the government. These tenders or currencies issued by governments or government-owned banks were similar in nature to a banknote; i.e. they are promissory notes linked to gold. This came to be known as the gold standard. This changed in the twentieth century when the linkage of money to gold was broken by many governments. Now money has value only because people ascribe value to it, not because a commodity or anything tangible for that matter backs it. Nevertheless, the link between money and banks remained.

---

[1] Paine, T. and Foner, P. S. (ed.) (1945). *The Complete Writings of Thomas Paine*. United States: Citadel Press. Vol 2, Page 411.

Even though private banks do not issue currency notes anymore, they still are closely linked to the money supply in an economy as they provide accounts that can be used for issuing checks. The relationship between banks and money needs to be understood very closely. Let us take an example in which a baker (A) produces a batch of bread and sells to a customer (C) for $100. Let us say this $100 is the only amount of currency floating in the economy. Let us say the baker deposits the currency in a bank (B) and then C goes to the bank and borrows $80 for further consumption. The total currency circulating is still $100, $80 with C and $20 with bank B. But the total money in the market is much more as the baker also assumes that he can draw his money any time and hence he assumes he has $100 with him. The total money circulating in the system is $180 ($100 of the baker's deposit and $80 of currency with C). The bank seems to have created money out of thin air. This is a feature of the fractional reserve banking system prevalent in most countries. In a fractional reserve banking system, only a part of deposits of a bank needs to be kept as cash reserve by the bank, the rest of it can be given out as loans. Thus the total amount of money in a system is much more than actual cash in the system. For example, if the banks are mandated to keep 5% of deposits as reserves and lend out the rest, then the rest 95% of the deposits will come back to the banking system as deposits. Of this 95 %, banks can again lend out further 95% so on and so forth. Mathematically if all money is kept as deposits in banks (and not kept as physical cash by customers) then:

Total Money in Deposits = Total Cash in Circulation / Reserve Requirement

Where the denominator (Reserve Requirement) is 5% or 0.05 in the above example. So the total money in the form of deposits is 20 times the cash in the economy. In the real world, the multiplier is much less than 20 (maybe close to 4) as not all money is deposited into the bank system and banks may not give out loans to the fullest extent allowed. Thus we have two types of money with different definitions: one being physical cash (coins, bills, and checking accounts) and the other being deposits in banks. The first type of money is called M1 and M1 together with the second type of money is called M2 (usually only savings deposits and retail time deposits are taken and not large long term deposits)[2]. Issuing and taking away cash from the economy can control M1. M2 can be controlled by controlling M1 and also by changing reserve requirements to be kept against deposits, but the movement in M2 is not linked to the movement in M1 on a one to one basis. The ratio between M2 and M1 depends on how much credit banks are giving out. If banks decide to hold on to more cash or central bank reserves than give out loans they decrease the supply of M2 money. This strong linkage of money supply and the banking system is one of the reasons banks are regulated by the central bank.

Monetarism

Although the history of money itself is very fascinating, it was not until the start of the twentieth century that money became the most important tool for economic control. Until then, money was mostly linked to a precious metal like gold. At the start of the twentieth century, we saw glimpses of monetarism - the economic policy of managing inflation and other economic parameters through money supply, which will eventually become the most important tool governments across the world use to control the pace of the economy. The first signs of establishment of the modern monetary system came about with the establishment of central banks, with monopoly rights on issuing currencies. This happened in the middle of the 19th century in the UK. In the US, this was attempted several times in the late 18th century and the 19th century, without success, but eventually, it was achieved with the establishment of the Federal Reserve System in 1913. Most countries established their own central bank and monetary system in the first half of the 20th century. Having a central bank as a liquidity provider was seen as an important aspect of managing financial crises. Although initially envisaged as just a liquidity provider, the role of the Federal Reserve System (or the Fed) increased gradually over time.

After World War I, the Fed gained the power to create and destroy money, thus establishing a monopoly on US dollars. During the 1920s the Fed experimented with the newly gained powers by creating and destroying money as per its understanding of the need for money. The increase in money supply towards the end of the 1920s caused asset prices (especially stock

---

[2] The definition of what constitutes M2 deposits changes from country to country. In the US, M2, as defined by the Federal Reserve, consists of M1 and (1) savings deposits (2) small-denomination time deposits (fixed term deposits in amounts of less than $100,000) and (3) balances in retail money market mutual funds. Investments as part of individual retirement accounts (IRA) and tax deferred pension accounts (Keogh accounts) are excluded.

prices) to be overvalued and this led to the crash of 1929 and the subsequent prolonged depression in economic activity aptly named the Great Depression.

The linking of currencies to the value of gold got a severe blow during the Great Depression. Several countries in Europe could not keep their currencies pegged to the value of gold as the demand for gold increased drastically. These countries devalued their currencies or let go of the gold standard. Even the US devalued the US dollar in 1934 from a value of $20.67 for one ounce of gold to $35 for one ounce of gold. But the gold standard remained in force for the US dollar (at a devalued level) until 1973, when it was let go, as it was not consistent with monetarism[3]. Monetarism gained significant popularity after the decoupling of the currency and gold, as the Fed can now easily increase or decrease the money supply. The decoupled currencies would be called fiat currencies. Fiat is a Latin term meaning "let it be done". Fiat currencies do not have intrinsic value but have value only because the government decrees that they have value and thus the government has a monopoly on fiat currencies.

In the 1970s, faced with stagflation (economic stagnation and inflation together), economists moved away from Keynesianism and latched onto the new framework of monetarism championed by Milton Friedman. Keynesianism is an economic theory that recommends that the government should use spending as a means to boost demand and hence the growth of an economy. Keynesians believe demand is the primary driving force in an economy and hence they support the expansionary fiscal policy to boost the economy. Its main tools are government spending on infrastructure, unemployment benefits, and education. Expansionary fiscal policies being interventionist in nature distort the market and tend to increase inflation as it happened in the 1970s.

To fight inflation, Milton Friedman recommended managing inflation through money supply. He attributed the inflation to high levels of money supply. He famously said, "inflation is always and everywhere a monetary phenomenon."[4] His argument is that as the level of money supply goes up in an economy, the inflation goes up with it[5]. Monetarist arguments led to an increase in interest rates in the US to control the money supply and fight inflation in the 1970s. Tight control of money supply with large scale reforms

[3] Elwell, C. K. (2011). "Brief history of the gold standard in the United States." Fas.org (Congressional Research Service) [Web]. Retrieved from: https://fas.org/sgp/crs/misc/R4 1887.pdf.

[4] Friedman, M. (1994). *Money Mischief: Episodes in Monetary History.* United States: Houghton Mifflin Harcourt. Page 49.

[5] Friedman, M. and Schwartz, A. J. (1963). *A monetary history of the United States, 1867-1960.* Princeton: Princeton University Press. Page 49.

and deregulation carried out in the 1980s in the US (by Ronald Reagan's administration) and in the UK (by Margaret Thatcher's administration) have led to a revival of economic growth. In the process of fighting inflation and controlling the money supply, central banks gained more power. Although originally money supply measures were intended to only manage inflation, central banks over time started using it as a tool to boost the economy as well. Central banks continue to exercise this power to date (as of 2020).

Modern innovations in monetary policy are mainly driven by the Federal Reserve (the Fed) of the United States. Hence I will discuss monetary policy with the Fed as a focus but the insights are applicable equally to any other monetary system. Most monetarists including Milton Friedman argued that central banks should solely focus on price stability. Classical economists believe that the level of the money supply does not have an effect on real values like real GDP and employment in the long term. Nevertheless, the Fed started using monetary policy actively to target employment and growth, most significantly during the governorship of Alan Greenspan (1987-2005) and subsequently. This has led to monetarism becoming the main tool for managing macroeconomic targets. Other central banks around the world typically followed the framework set by the Fed.

Until 2007, monetary policy mainly meant using interest rates to manage the supply of money. Interest for borrowing short-term money (typically overnight) by banks who are part of the monetary system, is controlled by the central bank of the country. The interest rates that are set/targeted by the central bank typically are the rates of borrowing excess funds deposited with the central banks or borrowing against the collateral of government bonds. As short term borrowing rates for banks go down or up, the lending rates of banks in the market also move accordingly. The interest rates are reduced by the central bank when inflation and employment rates are below the targets and interest rates are increased when inflation and employment rates are above the targets of the central bank. Usually, the government sets the targets of inflation and employment rate for the central bank to manage the economy. The graph in Figure 6.1. shows the trend of Fed fund rates - the rates at which banks borrowed Federal Reserve funds. Interest rates in other countries, especially in developed countries, follow a similar trend.

After the financial crisis of 2008, interest rate reduction was not sufficient to nip the downward trend of bankruptcies. This led to a new tool being introduced by the Fed and other central banks around the world to counter the liquidity crisis. The central banks, in addition to controlling short-term interest rates, started buying other assets to inject liquidity into the system. This tool came to be known as Quantitative Easing. There were several rounds of Quantitative Easing (QE) starting in 2008 all the way to 2020. Even after a long period of secular increase in the money supply through QE, the inflation in the US and across the world did not pick up. This brings into question the fundamental premise of monetarism that money supply and inflation are linked on a one to one basis. Growth and employment rates have recovered from the lows of 2008 and 2009, but they did not increase to the extent of the increase in the money supply. It can be argued that monetary policy is not as effective as it is thought out to be to manage macroeconomic targets.

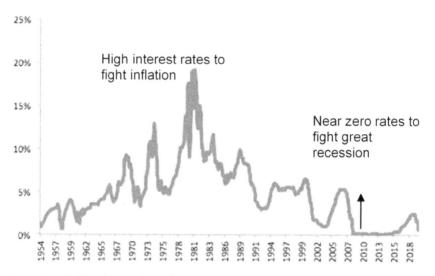

Figure 6.1. Fed Fund Rates Through the Years
Data Source: Federal Reserve Bank of St Louis[6]

Quantitative Easing helps in keeping interest rates low even when the government is borrowing more and more. In a crisis, when a government expands its fiscal deficit to give a fiscal stimulus to the economy, it needs to borrow more from the market. In a natural course, this should make borrowing more expensive for the government. But if the central bank buys a big portion of the bonds issued by the government, the cost of borrowing for the government will remain low. This is a roundabout way of printing money

---

[6] Federal Reserve Bank of St. Louis (2020). *Effective federal funds rate.* StLouisFed.org [Web]. Retrieved from: https://fred.stlouisfed.org/series/FEDFUNDS.

and giving it to the government and can eventually lead to distorted markets and high inflation[7].

A criticism of monetarism

Monetarists have been the champions of free-market economics, supporting classical views on various aspects of economics. They staunchly opposed Keynesian style interventions by the government to stimulate or cool the economy. Given this, it is surprising that monetarists missed seeing the fact that intervention in money markets by the government also interferes with the free market. In fact, monetarism can be seen as a form of Keynesianism to the extent that both believe that government intervention can help the economy. Where Keynesianism believes intervention in the form of government spending can help the economy, monetarism believes intervention in the money market can help the economy. True economic libertarians disagree with this. Hayek, the Austrian economist, in fact, says – "Milton and I agree on almost everything except monetary policy."[8] Of course, government interventions in the money market have an effect on the economy, but it is not necessarily true that that effect is good or equitable. Any form of intervention helps the entity receiving the money directly more than others in the economy. This creates distortions in various markets and inappropriate allocations of capital.

The main justification of using monetary policy was that it could be an effective tool to control liquidity crises as also inflationary scenarios. Milton Friedman argued that the Great Depression could have been avoided if the Fed provided enough liquidity to the banks as soon as the crisis started. He also argued that money supply could be used to increase or decrease inflation as per economic targets. In this context, he claimed through elaborate research that money supply had a direct bearing on inflation and the GDP (Gross Domestic Product). He used the equation of exchange to justify this relationship. The equation of exchange, formalized by Irving Fisher, states that Money supply (M), price of goods (P), and quantity of goods (Q) are linked through the equation:

---

[7] An emerging theory known as Modern Monetary Theory combines monetary policy (money supply) and fiscal policy (government spending and taxation) and states that the central bank can directly create money and give to the government for spending on stimulus programs. The risks of such a policy include future inflation especially the possibility of hyperinflation.

[8] Kresge, S. and Wenar, L. (eds.) (1994). *Hayek on Hayek: An autobiographical dialogue.* London: Routledge. Page 144.

$$M \times V = P \times Q$$

Where V is the velocity of money, i.e. the average frequency with which a unit of money is spent in a year. So if a dollar on an average is spent three times in a year then V is 3. This equation is a mechanical equation, the left side is the total amount of money spent on transactions and the right side is the total value of the transactions. Using this equation, monetarists argue that any increase in money supply will automatically translate into an increase in P (price levels) or Q (quantity of goods and services exchanged), as long as the velocity of money remains constant. PxQ is the total value of all transactions, and it is related to the nominal GDP (gross domestic product). On the face of it, this is a logical conclusion but the assumption of constant velocity cannot be ignored. As can be seen in the chart below, the velocity of money is not constant at all and keeps changing based on other economic factors. The graph in Figure 6.2. shows the velocity of M2 money in the US. The velocity of money in other countries will be equally volatile.

Figure 6.2. The Velocity of M2 Money in the US
Data Source: Federal Reserve Bank of St Louis[9]

[9] Federal Reserve Bank of St. Louis (2020). *Velocity of M2 money stock.* StLouisFed.org [Web]. Retrieved from: https://fred.stlouisfed.org/series/M2V.

In fact, it can also be argued that the velocity of money does not have any independent meaning other than being defined by the equation of exchange. Thus one can argue that the velocity of money is determined by P, Q, and M as they move independently driven by other factors. Thus money supply does not have a direct relationship with price level and output in an economy.

So the immediate question is what affects the price level (consequentially inflation) in an economy? The answer can come from the "subjective theory of value" propounded by Austrian economists, most prominently by Carl Menger at the end of the 19th century and the start of the 20th century. Menger's great insight was that the value of a good does not depend on any inherent quality of the goods nor the amount of labor/raw material used to produce the goods; rather it depended on how much value humans subjectively assigned to the goods based on their needs, views, sentiments, etc.[10] The market reflects these values in terms of prices. Thus a diamond is much pricier than let's say water not because of the labor of obtaining the diamond but because of the value humans ascribe to it. The same logic can be applied to money - humans determine the value of money subjectively. As the value ascribed subjectively to money goes up the price of goods comes down and as the value of money comes down the price of goods goes up. In other words, inflation is nothing but an outcome of movement in the value subjectively assigned by humans to money. Thus rather than being a monetary phenomenon, inflation mostly seems to be a subjective phenomenon. This explains the fact that increasing money supply has not induced high inflation in the last decade - because of flight to quality, humans have started ascribing more and more value to liquid money as opposed to other assets, thus putting a cap on inflation. This also explains the significant drop in the velocity of money in the first two decades of the 21st century. As can be seen in the wide fluctuation of the velocity of money, the relationship between money supply and inflation is not one to one as assumed by monetarists.

Monetarism, apart from being ineffective in controlling inflation or managing growth, can also have distortionary impacts depending on how the monetary policy is implemented, as money given out will help the person who receives the money first the most. If there is a banking crisis and money is given out to banks by lending them money at cheap rates then it might help avoid bankruptcies in the banking sector. But how much of that benefit is transferred to the rest of the economy is debatable even though economists assume that there will be a trickle-down effect. Similarly, if monetary policy is

---

[10] Menger, C., Dingwall, J. (trans.), and Hoselitz, B. F. (trans.) (1994). *Principles of economics*. Grove City, PA: Libertarian Press.

implemented through purchase and sale of bonds when the central bank increases the money supply by the purchase of bonds it helps the bondholders the most.

Another big problem with monetarism is that it does not advocate complete freedom in the most important markets - the money market. Free markets allow efficient allocation of resources. Any intervention in free markets by the government creates a distortion in this process. A few people (as part of a central bank or any other institution) will not have complete information to take efficient and immediate actions. If there is a slowdown in the economy or if there is a possibility of a slowdown, the money market left to itself will correct and the interest rates will come down. If inflation is picking up, the interest rates will automatically go up in a free market. Interest rates will go up if inflation goes up because the value of money today will be much more than the value of money in the future. The interest rates will move to the extent that they achieve a level where both borrower and lender will benefit. This may not be the case when the central bank fixes the interest rates. If the interest rates are not set at a market-clearing level, one of the parties - lender or borrower - will be at a disadvantage. Same goes with quantitative easing, one of the parties will be at a disadvantage. With quantitative easing, entities that already have accumulated assets will be at an advantage compared to entities that want to save and invest in the future. This creates inequity and distortion, typically giving the advantage to the rich over the poor. For the principles of liberty to hold, money markets like any other market should be allowed to operate freely. Just as buying and selling of gold are not controlled (at least in most economies), borrowing or lending of money should also not be controlled/manipulated. It is very strange that monetarists miss this point about freedom of markets.

Managing the money supply by the government also faces the practical problem that the money supply is not accurately defined. The amount of money in the system depends on the definition of money. We have already seen two definitions of the money supply- M1 and M2. There could be several other definitions of money like money including long-term deposits with banks and deposits in non-banking institutions. Change in each of these "types" of money can have different effects on the economy. This makes monetary policy all the more complicated and less effective. The money supply for the US in terms of M2 and M1 (as defined above) is shown in the graph below. As can be seen in Figure 6.3., the ratio of M2 to M1 is not constant but keeps changing. Increasing M1 does not have a completely predictable increase in M2.

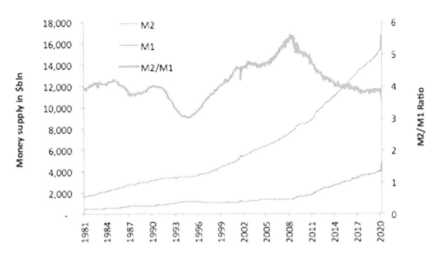

Figure 6.3. Money Supply in the US
Data Source: Federal Reserve Bank of St Louis[11]

With the development of technological innovations like instantaneous (real-time) money transfers, digital wallets, and cryptocurrencies, precise management of money supply will become even tougher.

Changing role of central banks

Central banks are the key institutions for maintaining the monetary systems of countries. Central banks across the world have been set up for various reasons: to fund the government, to act as liquidity providers to banks, to act as lenders of last resort, and to mint/print money. Over time, almost all of these roles have been taken up by each of the central banks across countries. The Bank of England was for example set up as an institution to lend to the government of England. The Federal Reserve was set up as a lender of last resort and liquidity provider to the banks in the US. European Central Bank was set up to issue Euros and manage the supply of Euros. Currently, all three of these institutions, and many other central banks across the world, have assumed a broadly similar set of roles. Broadly these roles can be categorized as:

---

[11] Federal Reserve Bank of St. Louis (2020). *M1 money stock*. StLouisFed.org [Web]. Retrieved from: https://fred.stlouisfed.org/series/M1.
and
Federal Reserve Bank of St. Louis (2020). *M2 money stock*. StLouisFed.org [Web]. Retrieved from: https://fred.stlouisfed.org/series/M2.

- Maintaining reserves of banks that are part of the monetary system

- Managing short term borrowing rates in the market

- Injecting liquidity through buying of securities à la Quantitative Easing

- Regulating the banking sector

- Supervising the risks in the banking sector

Other than these there are some specific roles certain central banks take upon themselves, including managing the payments infrastructure of the country, minting, and printing of money, maintaining foreign exchange reserves of the country, controlling and regulating foreign exchange trade. Sometimes central banks also bail out specific banks or take an active part in bailing out. As the central banks support banks in times of crisis, they also monitor the banking system for potential risks.

Although the Fed started with a simple idea of providing liquidity when required so that the economy functions smoothly, it significantly diverted from this goal over the course of its 100 years of existence. To start with, the Fed assumed the role of managing money supply in the economy. Slowly over time, it took on the responsibility of controlling inflation through interest rate changes, as a result of the popularity of monetarism. Towards the end of the 20th century, it took the additional responsibility of managing the unemployment rate and growth as well. As an extension to this, post the financial crisis of 2008, the Fed started taking the role of saving banks from bankruptcy - in other words acting as a judge of which business needs to survive and which does not. Most of the central banks across the world have followed a similar evolution story.

Having multiple roles and targets can reduce the efficacy of a central bank and there is a need to segregate these roles. Specifically, the role of price stability (i.e. controlling inflation) and the role of lender of last resort need not be taken up by a single entity. At times, both of these roles can conflict with each other. Historically, both of these roles have been executed by a single entity (i.e. the central bank) because of the fractional reserve banking system, where banks keep only part of the deposits as a reserve and lend the rest of the deposits in the processes creating new money. As a result of a fractional reserve banking system, regulation of banks and managing money supply have become dual roles of central banks. But having segregated roles can lead to better management of each of them with specific targets. The lender of last resort can help save the banking system in the event of crisis and can also regulate the banks based on the risk they carry. The lender of last resort can be independent of the government, in fact, it can be a privately formed entity where all banks can become members and contribute capital for providing the protection. This entity can manage the micro aspects of the banking system including risk monitoring of banks, providing emergency liquidity to a specific bank when required. This entity can assess each bank and take upon itself the credit risk of lending to banks needing liquidity.

There can be another entity that can manage the money supply and the effects of the same through open market operations. The second entity can manage the macro aspects of the economy through open market operations. For the lack of a better word, let us call this entity Monetary Authority. As there is no banking role for this entity, the name need not have the word "bank" in it. Monetary Authority should ideally not take any credit risk and should manage money supply only through buying and selling government securities or other risk-free instruments (like for example deposits with the Monetary Authority itself). Every other form of risk-taking should be left to the private entities in the markets. The intervention in the money market should be minimal and very transparent. The actions to be taken by this entity should be rule-based. Rule-based monetary policy can take away the discretion that central banks enjoy today. This can reduce uncertainty in money markets and remove distortions. There are several frameworks for setting up rules, which can be implemented by the Monetary Authority. In fact, as the rules mature, an automated algorithm can replace them. This idea is not new and has been in fact promoted by Milton Friedman. There could be several ways of setting the rules and as long as they are implemented transparently, the market can take care of allocating other resources efficiently. Friedman's rule, called the k-percent rule, suggests that the total money supply should be increased constantly every year at a fixed percentage[12]. Another popular rule, propounded by John B. Taylor, recommends that the short term interest rates should be set using a simple mathematical equation linked to the gap between inflation and GDP compared to targeted inflation and GDP[13]. It does not matter what rule is used as long as it is transparent and tamper-proof. The market will adjust to the rule automatically. As discussed earlier, the relationship between money supply and economic variables is very shaky and subjective in nature, so having the simplest of rules to manage monetary

---

[12] Friedman, M. (1960). *A Program for Monetary Stability*. New York City: Fordham University Press.

[13] Taylor, J. B. (1993). "Discretion versus policy rules in practice." Carnegie-Rochester Conference Series on Public Policy, Elsevier. Vol. 39(1).

policy is the best action to avoid distortions. Again to reiterate, it is not that monetary policy has no impact on the economy. It does. For example, the lowering of interest rates increases the value of assets. So people who own equities, bonds, or real estate will benefit. Similarly, people who do not own those assets, but are looking to invest in them for future income will be at a loss. Any trickle-down of this effect to the overall economy will be delayed and partial at best. Thus it is best to follow a very simple rule for monetary policy.

To conclude, the role of a central bank should be curtailed and instead of focusing on price stability and other targets, it should be split into two entities: one to support banks for liquidity needs and one to manage money supply mechanically through a rule-based framework. Money has existed independently without banks for a long time and it can continue to do so. There is no need to tie the banking system and money together. Of course, the banking system may need a regulation mainly because of the interests of small depositors, but the regulation needs to be done through a risk-based supervision framework. This framework, which is being advocated strongly by the Bank of International Settlements, can be implemented by the liquidity providers as they are the ones who will act as lenders of last resort. The lender of last resort need not be a government agency but can be set up as a private entity. This path can eventually lead to the complete abolishment of a central bank.

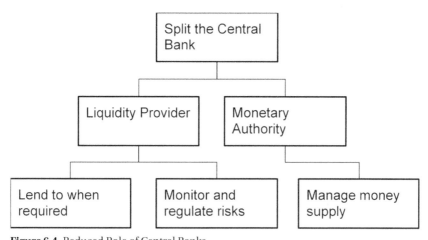

Figure 6.4. Reduced Role of Central Banks

Monetarists argue that having an independent and strong central bank can stabilize the economy. But this does not come with any evidence. In the over hundred years of existence of central banks across the world, we have seen a great depression, several recessions, a prolonged period of stagflation, and a financial crisis that resonated across the world. Along with this, asset price elevation as a result of quantitative easing is exacerbating income inequality. Central banks seem to be becoming part of the problem than of the solution. The time has come to question their raison d'être.

Monopoly on money

Even with a reformed central bank, where monetary policy is reduced to a rule, or with the abolishment of the central bank altogether, the currency still remains the monopoly of the government. As we have been saying again and again any monopoly by the government will lead to inefficient allocations and hinders growth. Hayek, in the book *Denationalisation of Money*, argues that a single national currency goes against the principles of the free market. He says that language, law, and money have been the pillars of our civilized society[14]. Both language and law have been continuously evolving to the needs of society. But the evolution of money has stopped after governments took over the supply of money and put a restriction on developing new forms of money. When money was linked to gold, the governments had little influence on it. When banks started issuing notes as a substitute for coinage, it was a free market and everyone could choose to accept or reject a particular bank's notes. As central banks took over the supply of money and governments decreed that only the official currency can be used for making transactions, the innovations in money stopped. Having a single currency meant that business cycles are closely linked to that currency. On top of it, if the government or its agencies manage the currency, the cycles get more severe.

Having a monopoly on currency issuance meant that governments now need not worry about their expenditures, they can always print more money or borrow it from the central banks. As a result, budgets of governments become unrestrained, leading to the formation of big governments. A monopoly on money helps government tax individuals indirectly through the inflation tax. In fact, emerging theories like Modern Monetary Theory (MMT) ask governments to take advantage of this monopoly directly by printing more and using the money as they deem fit. Indirectly even today governments are doing the same thing through the intervention of central banks. According to Hayek and most Austrian economists, this is what causes boom-bust cycles. Hayek also argues that having a single currency per country creates economic nationalism - countries trying to create a protective environment by enforcing restrictions on

---

[14] Hayek, F. A. (1990). *Denationalisation of money - The argument refined.* London: Institute of Economic Affairs.

currency conversions. All of these defects - inefficiency, lack of restraint on government expenditure, economic protectionism, and even inflation, can be cured by removing the monopoly on money. There has been increased attention to these aspects after the crisis of 2008 and subsequent governmental actions.

At this point, it is worthwhile considering the counterpoint of MMT proponents, who argue that rather than controlling the monopoly on money, the government should exploit the monopoly and increase the monetary base to fund the deficits directly. According to the supporters of MMT, budgetary constraints do not apply to countries that have their own fiat currency. They contend that the government's budget should not be treated on the lines of a household budget as governments can print their own money. They argue that the theory will work for the US and other developed countries as well for emerging countries. Creating new money to finance the debt of the government is called debt monetization. Conventional economists, both Keynesians and Monetarists alike, oppose these kinds of policies. That is ironic given the fact that they advocate measures equivalent to debt monetization, although in a surreptitious way, where the government issues debt in the market and the central bank buys the debt from the market. Although MMT is gaining prominence in academic circles only recently, it has been practiced by various countries to fund their budget deficits in the past. The most notable application of MMT has been in Latin America where countries including Argentina, Bolivia, Brazil, Chile, Ecuador, Nicaragua, Peru, and Venezuela used ideas similar to that of MMT to finance their deficits by directly increasing the money supply. The most recent experimentation in MMT is in Venezuela starting in 1998 and continuing to date (as of 2020). Unconstrained budgets have led to unbounded fiscal and accompanying monetary expansion in these countries. The result of this expansion has been a crisis of currency, where people lost faith in the currency. Venezuela saw an onset of hyperinflation starting in 2015 with inflation exceeding 60,000% by 2018[15]. The high inflation, coupled with other factors, has caused severe unemployment and massive migration out of the country. This case study should act as a cautionary tale of what happens when a government misuses the monopoly on money. I do agree with MMT that, currently, money is a monopoly of the government; I do not agree with it on the prescription that this monopoly should be used for funding deficits. In fact, in the interest of liberty, governments should let go of this monopoly.

---

[15] International Monetary Fund (2020). *Inflation rate, average consumer prices. Annual percentage change.* IMF.org [Web]. Retrieved from: https://www.imf.org/external/data mapper/PCPIPCH@WEO/VEN.

So, what is the alternative if the government does not keep a monopoly on money? On careful observation, we can notice that money need not be created as a legal tender by the government. Like language and other standards, society can come up with private money that can be accepted. The only thing the government needs to do is to remove the restriction of creating new types of money. Citizens should be allowed to use any form of money they want. The parties in the transaction could determine the money used in a particular transaction. If I carry US Dollars in India and a street vendor is ready to accept US Dollars, I should not be restrained from using them. The argument need not be restricted to currencies issued by sovereigns, it can be extended to currencies issued privately as well. If a bank or a financial technology company issues its own currency and can get enough customers to accept it, there shouldn't be a restriction on that. This can bring in competition and the best currency could be accepted by a large population.

Privately issued currencies can be distinguished based on the monetary policy adopted (i.e. how the supply is managed) and also on technological merits like how can they be secured from theft and how can they be transferred easily. A big part of the acceptability of the currency is branding and marketing of the currency along with the issuer. Thus if a renowned entity with credible background issues a currency or if there is a strong brand built around the currency there is a higher chance of the currency being accepted.

A very special category of currencies issued by private entities consists of what are known as cryptocurrencies. Most famous of them being Bitcoin. A cryptocurrency (also called decentralized currency) is a digital token that can be used as a medium of exchange and it is secured through cryptographic technology. Transactions of cryptocurrencies, typically, do not use a central party that maintains the ledger of transactions (unlike in the case of fiat currencies where banks act as central parties maintaining ledgers). The ledger of transactions and hence the ownership of currencies is maintained in a decentralized fashion amongst various market participants. Cryptographic technology is used to ensure the ledgers are tamper-proof. Each cryptocurrency comes with its own set of features. The set of features includes algorithms for ensuring the security of the network, ease of transfer, ease of use - especially through other computer programs, speed of transfer, and most importantly the monetary policy or how the money supply is increased over time. Along with the rate of money supply, how the increased money supply is given out to the market participants is also a feature of the system. Typically, cryptocurrency systems give out currencies to people who process transactions, i.e. maintain the decentralized ledger. This acts as a motivation for processing transactions and maintaining the ledger. If more people participate in transaction processing, the system will become more robust. Bitcoin is the most popular and the first of the cryptocurrencies to appear. Bitcoin makes it easy to transfer money globally to anyone having a Bitcoin wallet. The transfer is cryptographically secured and it is maintained in a tamper-proof, decentralized ledger called a "blockchain". This innovation of having a decentralized ledger can have a disruptive effect on all activities closely linked to money. The true potential of the technology is yet to be achieved (as of 2020).

More than monetary aspects, the story of money has been one of technology. The first technological impact has been that of minting, which established minted coins as the primary form of currency rather than unminted metal. The next big change came about with the introduction of paper money. As paper is easy to transport, it replaced the heavy minted currencies. Then came plastic money with the advent of debit and credit cards, reducing the need for paper/physical money all the more. Digital platforms are the next logical innovations that came about at the start of this century. The next big technological impact on money is coming from cryptographic technologies. All technological innovations try to solve two problems with respect to money - how to make money easier to use and how to avoid counterfeiting/fraud. A combination of digital technology and cryptography is ideal for these purposes.

There is no clear winner yet in the non-fiat currencies, but having a currency free from the government seems inevitable. Non-fiat currencies could take any form - managed by a central counterparty, decentralized, pegged to some commodity, free-floating, etc. There are experiments by entrepreneurs on all of these fronts, but the jury is not out yet on what could scale in the market. Governments will have to redesign their policies around the phenomenon of non-fiat currencies. For long, governments, even the countries with freest markets, have suppressed the liberty to use a currency of one's choice. This has to change. I would like to conclude with a quote from F. A. Hayek -

"If only one kind of money is permitted, it is probably true that the monopoly of its issue must be under the control of the government. The concurrent circulation of several currencies might at times be slightly inconvenient, but careful analysis of its effects indicates that the advantages appear to be so very much greater than the inconveniences that they hardly count in comparison, though unfamiliarity with the new situation makes them appear much bigger than they probably would be." [16]

---

[16] Hayek, F. A. (1990). *Denationalisation of money - The argument refined.* London: Institute of Economic Affairs. Page 111.

Chapter 7

On universal basic income

I am now convinced that the simplest approach will prove to be the most effective — the solution to poverty is to abolish it directly by a now widely discussed measure: the guaranteed income.[1]

- Martin Luther King Jr

In all the chapters until now, I have been arguing for letting the free market do its job without the intervention of the government. That should create growth in the economy and also take care of income redistribution most efficiently. There is no need for any special incentives or subsidies or any other kind of interventionist mechanisms needed to bring markets to efficiency. Social justice should be automatically achieved in the *long run*. Therein lies the rub - in the long run we are all dead. As discussed earlier, market equilibrium is a dynamic process, and at all stages, the market is continuously striving towards equilibrium without ever achieving it. Thus, in the short term, some people may not achieve all the benefits of a free market economy. For such people a safety net from society is important. It should be ensured that this short-term impact does not have a long-term impact like death, permanent damage to health, not getting relevant skill training, etc. I have already talked about the role of the government in basic education and health care. But a safety net is beyond these two; it should include food, shelter, skill upgradation, and any other necessities, including entertainment, to lead a normal life and get back to employment. Each person has a unique set of needs and it does not befit the government to decide what are the basic needs of a person. It is more efficient and less distortionary to give out a certain amount of money for the unemployed/ underemployed and leave it up to the individual to choose how that money is spent. This is the fundamental argument behind universal basic income, where every citizen is assured of a minimum level of income - enough to cover basic needs, something like a "citizens' dividend". The difference between providing UBI and becoming a socialist/welfare state is that the basic income is only provided as a safety net and not to make every individual equal in

---

[1] King, M. L. (1967). *Where do we go from here: Chaos or community?*. New York City: Harper & Row. Page 162.

income/wealth. The motivation to earn more by providing valuable goods and services to society should not be taken away from the individual.

Universal basic income differs from other forms of welfare in that it is universal, unconditional, and automatic. UBI has to be given out universally to all citizens. In other words, it should not be restricted to a particular group of citizens, either filtered by geography, occupation, or any other such metric. In some implementations, basic income is given only to citizens whose income is below the basic income. In such cases, the basic income is called guaranteed minimum income. We will look at this nuance in detail later in this chapter. Other than being universal, UBI should also be given out unconditionally to the citizens without any restrictions on how the income is to be used. The citizen can decide for herself as to how she wants to spend the income. Lastly, UBI should be given out automatically as a right of the citizen without a need for the citizen to apply for the income. This reduces bureaucracy.

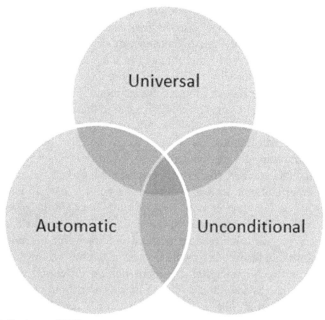

Figure 7.1. Features of UBI

The idea of unconditional universal basic income is not new. It was explored by the philosopher Sir Thomas More in his book Utopia in the 16th century. The idea could have been in existence for some time before that. Thomas More's close friend Johannes Ludovicus Vives should be credited for formalizing the idea of guaranteed income. Marquis de Condorcet and Thomas Paine, both prominent European republicans, further developed the idea towards the end of the 18th century. In the 20th century, great social philosophers including Bertrand Russell revived the idea. Even staunch free-market proponents have supported some kind of basic income. Milton Friedman was one of the supporters of UBI, although he advocated a slightly different version called negative income tax. His support to UBI gave it legitimacy amongst economic liberals of the US. Hayek was another proponent of UBI. Hayek in his Law, Legislation, and Liberty says - "The assurance of a certain minimum income for everyone, or a sort of floor below which nobody need fall even when he is unable to provide for himself, appears not only to be wholly legitimate protection against a risk common to all but a necessary part of the Great Society." [2]

The support for UBI has accelerated in the 2010s mainly driven by two factors. The first being economic and the second being technological. The financial crisis of 2008, has taught us that business cycles can have severe impacts on employment. Although this is not a new insight, the persistent recurrence of recessions that cause job losses despite active management of the economy by governments came as a surprise to many. In the turbulent times caused by boom and bust cycles, for many, UBI seems like an attractive option to have. On the technological side, swift technological changes like automation have caused certain jobs to be redundant and created the need for new kinds of jobs with new skills. Adapting to technological changes requires job seekers to acquire new skills, which takes time and money. UBI can support them on both these fronts. More recently, in 2020, UBI is being touted as a response for dealing with external shocks like pandemics. Several countries, including both developed and developing countries, have experimented with different forms of UBI. In the 1970s, experiments were conducted in the US and Canada. The 2010s saw some pilot programs of UBI in Finland, some countries in Africa, and some states in India. Most of these have remained as experiments and have not been implemented at a national scale. Alaska Permanent Fund is one of the few existing long-term implementations of UBI. This implementation has been funded by revenues from natural resources (oil). As the implementations are limited, the efficacy of UBI needs to be judged based on economic logic rather than actual data.

There are several ideologies that support UBI, including socialism and liberalism. Within the libertarian thought process, a subset called bleeding-

---

[2] Hayek, F. A. (1978). *Law, legislation and liberty*. Chicago: University of Chicago Press Economics Books. Page 55.

heart libertarianism strongly defends UBI alongside free-market policies.[3] Providing universal basic income is not incompatible with other free-market and minimal-government principles. From a libertarian perspective, UBI is justified mainly through three lines of argument: - as a moral duty of society, as a counter-action against past injustices, and as a better alternative to current welfare frameworks. Of course, there are libertarian objections to UBI - it disincentivizes work, it needs to be funded through taxes, etc. The positives outweigh the negatives and the implementation details of a UBI system have to be designed to mitigate some of the negative aspects of UBI. I will look at the justifications and the criticisms of UBI in more detail later in the chapter, but first, let us look at some of the libertarian arguments in favor of UBI.

UBI is a moral duty. I have spent a considerable amount of time discussing economic liberty, but if we go back to the start of the book, the motivation for economic liberty is to achieve universal prosperity. That is the end goal we want to achieve, although I haven't spent enough words on that. Economic policies are a path towards achieving that end goal. The justification for a need for universal prosperity and poverty reduction are moral in nature. Poverty affects human dignity severely and can have irreparable consequences including avoidable death. Hunger is the number one cause of death in the world. Hunger also causes stunted growth making an irrevocable impact on a person's future earnings. In addition to hunger, the poor are also affected by a lack of proper health care and education. It seems highly immoral to me to let a large population of our society be in poverty. Nearly half the world population lives on an income of less than $5.5 a day. Thus irrespective of whether one is a libertarian, is a socialist, is an interventionist, or is a Marxist, it is the moral obligation to keep poverty reduction, especially extreme poverty reduction as a primary goal for economic policies. As discussed in the chapter on economic liberty, economic principles do not come from a vacuum but from the objectives we want to achieve and from moral justifications. Even if non-intervention is a justified principle for achieving universal prosperity, UBI could be a much shorter path for reducing the effects of poverty than free-market mechanisms. No doubt, the poor can come to the job market and earn their incomes at the market-clearing rate and move out of poverty, but this process takes time and is contingent on several factors not under the control of the individual. For example, the skill sets and location of the job seeker and the employment opportunity need not match and poverty could do irreparable damage before suitable employment

---

[3] Zwolinski, M. (2013). "The libertarian case for a basic income." Libertarianism.org [Web]. Retrieved from: https://www.libertarianism.org/columns/libertarian-case-basic-income

is found. An interventionist approach of providing a minimum income on the other hand can quickly provide relief to the poor, give a helping hand to tide through the unemployment phase, and also provide enough time to upgrade the skills for suitable employment. Income guarantee can also help out the unemployable like the children. This creates a very strong moral justification to have some sort of income support for the poor even if such a step is interventionist in nature.

UBI is a correction for past injustice. Liberty to pursue one's own economic path goes hand in hand with justice and nonaggression. One cannot infringe upon others' rights in the process of acquiring income and wealth. Even if going forward, the rights are protected in a liberal economy, there is always the question of accumulated wealth that has been acquired through centuries and passed on to progeny. A large portion of wealth in the past has been acquired through means that might be considered unjust or violent in the current world. Land acquisition through wars, attaining monopoly through corruption, gaining income through employing serfs, etc. are all examples of these unjust practices of wealth acquisition. The counterpoint to this argument is that a lot of currently wealthy people need not have inherited wealth but may have created wealth during their lifetime, so why penalize them through taxes for paying UBI? Even if today's wealthy may not share the guilt directly, they are in part wealthy because of the accumulation of wealth over time, even if it is in small, incremental steps. Nevertheless, today's poor families have been most likely poor for several generations. These injustices can be corrected through universal basic income.

UBI is a better alternative. One of the main objections to a welfare state from free-market proponents, right after the objection that welfare can reduce the incentive to be productive, is that the state does not know what are the needs and requirements of each individual. One person may just need support on food and shelter, someone else may need money for learning new skills, someone else may need capital for investing in a trade, etc. Having a fixed set of welfare measures throttles this variety and puts curbs on the growth of individuals. Some of the other occupation-related subsidies that are given out by welfare states can distort markets. For example, several welfare countries tend to subsidize farming. This can lead to a distortion where citizens could stick to farming even if it is not a value-generating activity, rather than exploring more productive occupations. These citizens will require a continued subsidy for sustenance. Such distortions do not occur if an individual is provided basic income support not linked to specific occupation or usage. The individual can choose to use the income support the way they deem fit to maximize wealth and happiness over time. As UBI is non-distortionary and can be used for a variety of needs, it is a much better alternative to the current welfare programs that typically promote a certain type of consumption or occupation over others. On top of it, UBI, as it is a transfer of money, is much easier to administer compared to other forms of welfare where a significant amount of state machinery needs to get involved.

UBI might boost economic growth. The fallout of UBI on economic growth can be positive because of external effects on the overall economy. It is not right to argue that UBI will increase the GDP of an economy by increasing overall demand, as that rests on a Keynesian argument that demand does not fill all the supply. Nevertheless, there could be a positive impact of poverty reduction on the economy through increased production and productivity as a more able-bodied and skilled workforce will enter the economy if it is given the right opportunity to maintain good health and acquire relevant skills. UBI can move people employed at the lower end of the value chain to a higher level of the value chain. UBI can also abet entrepreneurship by reducing the consequences of failure. This can have a significant positive impact on the overall GDP of the country. The impact may not be immediately seen, as it takes time to improve capacities and absorb additional workforce but the impact can be long term and transformational.

UBI supports the liberty of the individual. UBI can provide a support system for people who do not want to pursue a job either temporarily or permanently. If a person wishes not to take up income fetching employment but wants to pursue non-income fetching goals, like for example arts and philosophy, UBI can support such a person's personal goals. If a person wants to get out of a particular job and sustain herself until she finds a better opportunity, even in such cases UBI can provide the support to do the same. This can be identified as an "emancipatory value". The emancipatory value can also promote gender equality. This argument comes with a double-edged sword though. Having a high amount of UBI can disincentivize work altogether, and hence can lead to a reduction in the overall productivity of the economy. Thus the level of UBI should be set such that it should give enough liberty to individuals but also leave enough motivation for more work and enterprise. As automation increases productivity of people and labor is no longer a constraint for production, the level of UBI can go up. I will come back to this further ahead in this chapter.

Let us also look at some of the negatives of UBI and how to counter them.

UBI could disincentivize work. Wages in an economy are an incentive mechanism for work and a feedback mechanism for the value of work. The argument against UBI goes like this - if wages are replaced with unconditional income, this could disincentivize people from working. This can also distort the labor market. Such distortions can have a negative impact on resource allocation and hence the overall economy. This is the most common argument against UBI. The disincentive will actually depend on the implementation of UBI though. A small amount of UBI enough for sustenance and other basic needs but not enough for a person for all the needs. Also, if the income is universal, then it is the person's to keep irrespective of having another job or not. So, working to get more money is not disincentivized. Nevertheless, the level of UBI should be just high enough to act as a safety net.

UBI has to be funded through taxes. I have argued that what a person produces as an output of labor belongs to that person alone. UBI runs contrary to this principle as one person's labor is taken away in the form of tax and given to another in the form of UBI. In a way, UBI is a forced charity. But we humans live in a society and are dependent on society for some of the income we generate, especially income that comes from land and natural resources. Sharing part of this income with the less privileged is not contrary to principles of natural justice. Funding for UBI through taxes is justified as UBI is a citizen's dividend for shared claims on the natural resources of a country. On top of it, if the government reduces all other welfare schemes, subsidies, and non-productive spending while providing UBI, the overall taxes could be reduced.

UBI is unaffordable for some countries. For some countries, where poverty is more prevalent and the tax collections are low, funding UBI can lead to large deficits putting pressure on government finances, which can lead to financial stress. This is a problem, especially with emerging economies. The concern is real, but the solution is not to shelve UBI but to incorporate other reforms along with UBI, including a reduction in overall subsidies/welfare, implementing the land tax, and reducing the size of the government. All of this cannot be done in a single day so it has to be a gradual process with UBI being implemented in stages - the level of basic income can be small initially and given out only to the poorest. Over time, as other reforms reduce the deficit of the government the level of UBI can increase and it can become universal.

UBI can be abused. It can be argued that UBI will be abused as it is given out unconditionally. Recipients can spend the UBI on alcohol and other abusive purposes rather than on food, healthcare, and education. Providing these services to citizens rather than giving them money can eliminate the chance of abuse. Although this is a social problem, it is a valid argument against UBI. Not everyone may prioritize short-term gratification over services that benefit in the long term, but there will be definitely a section of the recipients who will be doing so. An extreme case of this could be that a parent spends the family's basic income completely on oneself and does not spend anything on children's education. This problem can be avoided if certain absolutely necessary services like education for children and healthcare are kept outside the purview of UBI and provided as welfare through government administration or coupons that can be used for specific purposes. Other than that, we have to live with deficiencies and use awareness and education to solve some of these problems with the use of UBI. It will be a mistake to take away the benefit of UBI for a large segment of the poor just to avoid abuse by some.

UBI could lead to inflation. As UBI provides income to a certain set of people without a corresponding productive output, this can lead to inflation, especially if labor is a constraint in the production of goods and services. The total pie to be shared diminishes if a set of people move out of the labor force and if they still have the money for consumption, the prices for goods produced by the rest of the labor force will become more expensive. This can put marginally poor who are not eligible for UBI at risk of losing purchasing power. The problem is accentuated if a large set of labor force remains out of productive activity for a long time because of UBI. This again brings us to the ideal level of UBI - it should be enough for sustenance but not high enough to satisfy all the needs.

UBI may not be as easy to administer, as it seems on the face of it. One of the positive features of UBI that I have highlighted earlier is that it is easier to administer than current welfare schemes. That may not be a reality in practical terms if the UBI is not universally and automatically transferred to each and every citizen. If there are criteria put to identify recipients and to calculate the amount to be transferred then the administration of UBI could not be as easy. For example, if a country decides to pay only the poor and the payment is linked to the cost of living in the locality of the poor then there need to be several sets of rules to identify the poor and also to calculate the cost of living. In such scenarios, eventually, UBI rules could be as complex as the current tax codes in various countries. This will require additional bureaucracy to administer the UBI system, thus defeating the simplicity of UBI. This is a practical difficulty that needs to be overcome by making the UBI system as simple as possible. Keeping UBI universal may not be economically feasible for some countries, but it can be kept constant (not linking to location). Also, delegating the administration of UBI to local authorities reduces some of the administrative difficulties. We need to look at some of these practical aspects of implementing UBI in detail.

While designing the ideal UBI policy for a country, the main parameters that need to be considered include the type of income, the eligibility criteria, and the level of income. We need not decide the perfect implementation plan, as that could be different for each country, but we need to be aware of the options available.

Income type

If a fixed income is given out universally irrespective of the current income of the person, then it is called citizen's dividend (as it is a grant for being a citizen) or simply UBI. But, if it is not given out universally and is dependent on the income of the person there could be two variants of UBI: basic income guarantee (BIG) and negative income tax (NIT). In the case of BIG, the gap between a basic income and the actual income of the person is paid out to the person. If the person's income is above the basic income, no additional income is paid to the person by the state. In the case of a negative income tax, a certain uniform percentage of the gap between basic income and the actual income is paid out by the state. This percentage is called the negative income tax as it is paid by the state rather unlike taxes that are collected by the state. I will take an example where the basic income is set at $10,000 and look at three scenarios of three persons whose current incomes are $100,000, $8,000, and $2,000. Table 7.1. summarizes what each person will receive as income in different types of UBI implementation, we are assuming a negative income tax rate is 40%.

Table 7.1. Comparison of Various Income Types Alternative to UBI

		Income type: UBI	Income type: BIG	Income type: NIT
Person 1: Income of $100,000	Income from state	$10,000	-	-
	Total Income	$110,000	$100,000	$100,000
Person 2: Income of $8,000	Income from state	$10,000	$2,000	$800
	Total Income	$18,000	$10,000	$8,800
Person 3: Income of $2,000	Income from state	$10,000	$8,000	$3,200
	Total Income	$12,000	$10,000	$5,200

As can be seen, if the income is universal, the income is for the person to keep, irrespective of whether she works or not (I have not considered taxes but taxes do not affect the conclusions I'm about to draw). As a result, even with the UBI, the incentive to work is not taken away. Whereas, in the case of BIG, the income of the person increases only if that person makes more than the guaranteed income. In the above example, for the case of BIG, whether the person works to earn $2,000 or $8,000 she will be getting the same total income. This disincentivizes people from working unless they are able to earn much more than the minimum guaranteed income. This disincentive is not there in the case of NIT. As can be seen in the example, in the case of NIT, for a person earning $2,000 the total income is $5,200 whereas for someone earning $8,000 the total income is $8,800 - the income increases as the person earns more money in the case of NIT. Thus UBI and NIT are better options than BIG. UBI might be better from an operational standpoint as there is no need to assess the income of each person, on the other hand, it can be more expensive as all the population will be eligible for the income. Another option is to give a fixed amount for a subset of the population identified as poor. Here again, income assessment needs to be done, but it need not be very accurate. An easier way to implement universal income so that it benefits only the poor is to give the income universally and automatically to everyone and then recollect the given income in the form of tax based on tax returns from the rich.

Eligibility criteria

Irrespective of the type of income provided: fixed citizen's dividend, basic income guarantee, or negative income tax, the state can put some additional criteria on selecting who the income should be given to. Income level could be one criterion as we have seen. Other than that, age and gender could be other criteria. One option governments can consider is to give UBI only to women to promote gender equality. Another option governments can consider is to give UBI only to adults, assuming the cost of living for children will be subsumed within that. Governments can also consider giving income at a family level rather than to individuals. This can be discriminatory against larger families though. Governments can also consider giving different incomes for children and adults. Exact eligibility criteria should take into consideration the need of the individuals, the spending capacity of the government, and the ease of implementation.

Income level

I have alluded to the fact that the level of income paid as UBI should be high enough to support the sustenance of a person but not high enough to disincentivize further work and it should not be higher than what a country can afford. Ideally, it should be uniform and not linked to the location. Having a differential UBI based on location can cause perverse incentives to migrate. Differential UBI based on location is feasible only if it is funded and administered by local governments. The level of income needs to be determined to take into consideration all of these factors. To determine the level of basic income, we need to create an average basket of goods and services that are needed by people to sustain. These should at the minimum include food, shelter, healthcare, and basic education (if healthcare and education are not supported by other welfare schemes). The level of basic income should be reviewed periodically to assess inflationary effects.

Although a significant amount of thought has gone into UBI, it is still in the developmental stage. The impact of UBI in the real world is not known yet. From economic reasoning, the positives of having UBI outweigh the negatives. Details matter much more in this case, as this is an interventionist mechanism. In free market-driven institutions, the market prices provide feedback on optimal strategy. Whereas, in interventionist policies like the UBI there is no market-driven mechanism that can provide feedback on the right set of policies. Designing the ideal system would require a lot of experimentation through randomized controlled trials (RCTs). RCT is a type of scientific experiment, typically used in medicine, to identify the effect of particular intervention by allocating subjects randomly to two (in some cases more) groups where one group is administered the intervention and another is not. The experiment can clearly identify the effect of the intervention by observing the performance of both groups. The feedback from the experiment can be used to scale the intervention. RCTs have become popular in developmental economics to optimize interventions. RCTs are not needed in a fully free-market economy as the market automatically provides continuous feedback. But they are necessary for interventionist programs like welfare schemes and UBI. Ideal UBI systems for each country could be different depending on the country's fiscal status and also its citizens' work ethics and needs. Even if there is no consensus on the need for UBI and its implementation details, there is an increasing awareness about UBI. It will take several more years to conclude the effects of UBI on poverty reduction. But free markets coupled with a small government and UBI can address both economic growth and social justice in a focused manner. The sooner we start on this path, the faster we will be able to achieve poverty elimination.

Part 3: Periphery

Chapter 8

On decentralization

The way to have good and safe government, is not to trust it all to one;
but to divide it among the many, distributing to every one exactly the
functions he is competent to.[1]

- Thomas Jefferson

Decentralization and liberty are very closely linked to each other. From a political standpoint, decentralization starts by giving individuals the right to decide through democracy. On the economic front, decentralization helps free markets work better. The key reason for a free market to work better than centralized decisions by a government is that the market is aware of the needs and values driving each transaction in the economy. Decentralized forces make the market more efficient than a system with a single authority deciding the prices and quantities of goods and services in an economy. If this logic is extended, then it can be argued that where government intervention is necessary, especially in the scenarios discussed in the chapter on the role of the government, it is always better to have the intervention decentralized. The more power local governments have, the more efficient the government intervention will be, as the local governments will have much more information than the central government. This is especially true for large countries. On top of it, local governments can move faster. Each local government can decide specific policies based on local needs.

The principles of liberty that apply to individuals can be extrapolated to certain collective bodies. The next level of unit after an individual is a family, then a community or a town, then comes the county or state and at the top of the hierarchy is the nation. The liberty accorded to individuals should flow upwards. A family should have more liberty than a town, a town should have more liberty collectively than a county, and so forth. If there is a collectivist intervention required, then it is best executed as close to the individual as possible. This forms the basis of the argument supporting decentralized

---

[1] Jefferson, T., Lipscomb, A. A. (ed.), and Bergh, A. E. (ed.) (1905). *The writings of Thomas Jefferson.* Washington, DC: Thomas Jefferson Memorial Association of the United States. Vol. 6, page 418.

decision-making. Increased centralization in business or government puts more power in a small set of people and this can cause inefficiencies because of various reasons like suboptimal decision making, corruption, moral hazards, etc. Only decentralization can remove such power from a single source. This makes decentralization fait accompli to liberty.

Humans lived a decentralized life in communities of about 100-200 people for a very long time. Only in the last ten thousand years of our existence, we have moved to a centralized society. The centralization was driven by the rise of agriculture. Having an agriculture driven economy required ownership of land and division of labor. Of course, this also led to an increase in productivity and wealth. As land became an important resource, political and economic institutions started getting built around it - like armies to protect land, etc. Slowly, societies started trusting central authorities for maintaining rights and defending the land. Increasingly, the local authorities, i.e. governments, started consolidating and became nations and empires. In our very long history of humanity, only less than 10,000 years have been in this centralization trend. Even after the establishment of kingdoms, there was sufficient decentralization arising out of fiefdoms and local counts/governors, etc. Big empires mostly only collected taxes and did not interfere much with local administration. Two counter-trends emerged in the last two centuries: one is democracy, where the citizens gained more power and the second is the increase in power of the national government. While democracy has added liberty, the bloating up of governments has curtailed the same. This centralization of power needs to be reduced to give citizens more liberty.

The first use of the term "centralization" emerged in France around the time of the revolution (late 18th century). The early 19th century saw the development of the idea of decentralization in governance, mostly in France. Decentralization soon became popular because it helped solve administrative problems and also gave more liberty to local authorities. 20th-century liberals have buttressed the arguments for decentralization. In the 20th century, along with growing democracies around the world, the support for more decentralized administration also grew. But as states got more involved in economic affairs with the pretext of national security, economic stimulus, or welfare, the same democracies became more centralized. Central governmental institutions gained more power during various economic and political shocks of the 20th century and they gave up little of the powers that they gained. By the end of the twentieth-century governments of most countries have become a top-down structure where the central government formulates and implements key economic policies like fiscal and monetary policies. States and local authorities had little control over taxation, spending, business regulation, and money supply, except in very few countries like

Switzerland and the United States where some autonomy of cantons/states still exists in economic matters.

Along with the centralization of the government, businesses also started getting centralized. A small number of institutions controlled the flow of information, money, and other services. Banks, for example, controlled virtually the flow of all money. Internet service providers controlled most of the information flow. This centralization in business ecosystems happened because of a move towards more efficiency. An example of a centralized business ecosystem is the banking system where transactions have to be routed through a single platform. Another example is a securities depository system where digitized securities (stocks, bonds, etc.) are held by a small number of entities called depositories. The cryptocurrency movement and associated technology of blockchain have brought back the focus on decentralization. Although these technologies help decentralize information and finance, there is a spillover of this movement on governance as well. The movement for decentralization had not picked up full steam yet though (as of 2020).

There is a difference in the way decentralization works in the government and business ecosystems. In the case of government, the role and hegemony of the central government of a country will remain how much ever power is delegated to local governments. In the case of business ecosystems, there is no need for any one party to be superior to others.

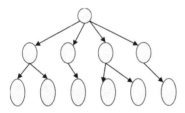

Decentralization in government: Small central government and more powerful local governments

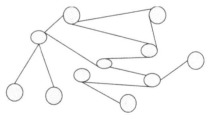

Decentralization in business ecosystems: No single entity has more power than others

Figure 8.1. Decentralization in Government and Business Ecosystems

I am not advocating for the busting of a large organization to replace it with smaller companies. This would be against the economic liberties that organizations have. But when business ecosystems get developed, the government or its agencies should not put any restrictions on using only centralized systems. The participants of the ecosystem should be able to choose their own methods to interact with others in the ecosystem. If a decentralized system is efficient and desirable in an ecosystem, market forces ensure that the ecosystem gravitates towards a decentralized system unless there are restrictions imposed by the government. On the other hand, with regards to the government, there is a need for explicitly making the structure decentralized as there are no competitive forces that can make the government gravitate towards decentralization.

Why decentralization?

Although I have made a case for decentralization based on principles of liberty, we need to look at the exact reasons why a decentralized system is better. The main reasons for the efficiency of decentralization are: it increases competition amongst different local bodies, it reduces corruptive influence, and it gives more power to the people with more information. Although this is true only if decentralization is implemented properly without adding to bureaucracy. Decentralization should reduce the number of layers in the decision-making process. If on the other hand more layers are added, for example, if a decision has to go through both local authorities and higher authorities in the government, it can only lead to more inefficiency and corruption. Whereas, if the decision-making is spread horizontally across various local bodies, the efficiency of decision-making will increase.

Firstly, having more entities with decision-making power automatically increases competition. This is true with governments and also with business ecosystems. In a business ecosystem, it is obvious that when centralized systems are broken, competition increases. If several clearinghouses can clear the money movement, then obviously they will compete with each other to give the best service at the cheapest cost. Even in the case of the government, if each of the local authorities has a decision making power then the local authorities can formulate their policies to attract businesses and also people (if required) to their jurisdictions. This can create a healthy competition amongst local authorities.

Secondly, it is easier for a centralized system to become corrupt because it will take only a few people to be corrupt. Corruption does not just mean preferring one person or entity to another for monetary gains. Corruption can also be in the form of misalignment of the objectives of the decision-maker and other stakeholders. All decision-makers, whether in the government or businesses, have a personal agenda be it popularity, reelection, power, or money. This can deviate from the overall objective of the people they represent. In such a scenario, the decision-makers can become corrupt and prioritize their own agenda. This problem is partly addressed in a decentralized system: several people need to become corrupt if the system has to deviate from its overall goal, as power is spread out.

Lastly, in a decentralized system, people who are the closest to the stakeholders make decisions. Local governments understand local issues better and have more information at a micro-level. Also, they have a more vested interest in serving the local citizens better as they will get voted out if their decisions are misaligned with the needs of their constituency. As a result, local governments will be able to make more appropriate decisions than a faraway government. The same can be said about business ecosystems as well. Decentralization could be a good idea in several different setups including let us say inside an organization. But I believe it is very crucial for three specific ecosystems to be decentralized - governance, information, and finance. These three ecosystems form the pillars of modern society. For a truly decentralized society, all of these ecosystems need to be decentralized. There are other ecosystems, like energy production, farming, manufacturing, etc., that are mostly decentralized or will be decentralized eventually because of market forces. Economies of scale are hindering decentralization, but as technology makes smaller businesses feasible these ecosystems will become more decentralized. I will look at this in the chapter on technology. But governance, finance, and information ecosystems are still centralized because of various restrictions imposed by the government.

Decentralization in governance

Governance in most countries is in an extremely centralized structure. In most countries - laws are enacted by central governments; taxation and budgetary allocations are decided by a central government; foreign affairs and international trade are governed by a central government. Local governments have some rights, but they are mostly used for delegating duties and implementation of national policies. Central governments typically use local governments as administrative tools and not as decision-making bodies. Governance involves both framing and implementation of policies/laws. Local governments should be able to do a wide variety of governing activities, including deciding tax rates, spending, and law and order. Within each local government also there could be further decentralization in terms of departments. A big catalyst of decentralization in governance is competition amongst nations to provide the most flexible environment for business. Because of this competition, nations are creating special economic zones that have more autonomy with their jurisdiction separate from the rest of the nation.

The nature of hierarchy and the levels in the hierarchy of a government will depend upon the size of the nation. Small city-states need not have elaborate hierarchies. Larger countries can have states within them. Each state can have counties/districts and each district can have municipalities/towns. Some anarchists go to the extent of arguing that there is no need for a hierarchy in the government at all, specifically there is no need for a central government. They argue that small, decentralized communities can come up with their own rules to interact with other communities and form a decentralized network rather than having top-down governmental structures. The arguments for an anarchist society are still in formative stages and there is no experimental evidence at the moment to support it. As of now, I believe a small government with more powers delegated to the lower levels of hierarchy could work better. This position is called "minarchism" sometimes.

For the decentralization of governance to be effective, most of the roles and aspects of governance should be delegated to lower levels. The central government can retain very specific roles that can only be administered centrally like monetary policy and national defense. All other aspects, including taxation, public goods, regulations, and welfare, should be decentralized to a large extent. We need to look at each of these in detail to identify what could be the role of central government vs. local governments. I want to highlight a framework that could be used to decide the roles of national and local governments. Actual implementation will depend on country-specific factors.

On taxation, I have discussed that from the liberal framework, only tax on land, natural resources (severance tax), pollution (Pigouvian tax), and a small corporate tax are justifiable. Any development work done in a locality by the local government directly benefits the landowners. Hence, local authorities should be the ones making policies around collecting and using land tax. In a single tax framework, land tax is the only income of the government. In such a case, part of the land tax will have to be passed on to the central government for defense and other expenses. Natural resources like mineral resources or water resources belong to local society and hence their usage should also be taxed by local authorities, but by a level above towns and municipalities. State or county government will be an ideal agency for taxing usage of natural resources. Pigouvian taxes should be collected by the central government as pollution cannot be typically localized. Nevertheless, part of the tax should be passed on to local governments as well. Corporate laws are typically established by a nation through central laws, so corporate taxes should be collected at a national level. Another reason for having a national tax on corporate profits is that, if there are differential taxes across the country for companies, companies can make shell companies in one locality even though they don't intend to run operations there. In addition to corporate taxes, the central government can also collect income taxes for very high-income individuals where the income reflects profits from a corporation, like bonuses, etc., and is not attributed purely to labor (as discussed in the chapter on taxation).

The role of government with regards to public goods can be split mainly into infrastructure development, national defense, and law and order. Infrastructure development and maintenance need not be the role of the government always. In specific cases, the market may not be able to deliver infrastructure because the market may not have the right of way. In such cases, the responsibility of infrastructure development will be split between national and local governments. Infrastructure can be national, like monetary systems, railways, and telecommunications or it can be localized like parks, water bodies, and roads. The former, where a right of way is required across states, will be the responsibility of the national government and the latter will be the responsibility of local government. National defense is another public good, this is the responsibility of the national government. National defense cannot be delegated to states or local governments as if it is left to the local bodies, some localities, that are not exposed to international threats, will freeride on other localities, like the border states. Law and order, on the other hand, is typically a local phenomenon, so it will be the responsibility of local governments. In the case of law and order, the only responsibility of the center would be to set up and run institutions that can help in coordination between states and resolve disputes between states.

I have argued that regulations on businesses should be minimal. Nevertheless, some regulations are inevitable. Such cases include businesses where there is a severe risk of life and property and businesses that have an impact on the environment and other natural resources. Any regulation related to local natural resources and land can be localized, but for other regulations, I believe the best way is for the center to formulate the policy - what to be regulated and how much. The states will be the ones who can implement the policies. This can make regulations uniform across the country and at the same time, make implementation easier. I have argued that only basic regulations need to be implemented. In such a case, there should not be much customization required for each state/city with regards to regulation.

The third important activity that governments take up is welfare. Welfare can be segregated as generic welfare schemes like universal basic income and specific areas like education and healthcare. I have argued that these three forms of welfare schemes should be enough to cover all the significant needs of a person. Food, shelter, etc. can be subsumed within a basic income scheme. As basic income is universal and uniform, it should be ideally administered by the center. Other forms of welfare, specifically healthcare and education are more interventionistic in nature and local authorities should implement them. Local authorities can take up further measures like shelters for the poor, food distribution, etc. if the basic income is not sufficient or there are specific requirements that cannot be fulfilled by the basic income.

Another way to bring about decentralization in governance is by designing an electoral system for central government in such a way that local concerns are better addressed. For example, instead of having large constituencies, one can have smaller constituencies (like for example at a council level) and these representatives can further elect representatives for the central government.

To sum up, I want to quote Thomas Jefferson, one of the founding fathers of the US, again - "Let the National government be entrusted with the defense of the nation, and its foreign and federal relations; the State governments with the civil rights, laws, police, and administration of what concerns the states generally; the Counties with the local concerns of the counties, and each Ward direct the interests within itself. It is by dividing and subdividing these republics from the great national one down thro' all its subordinates, until it ends in the administration of every man's farm and affairs by himself; by placing under every one what his own eye may superintend, that all will be done for the best." [2]

Decentralization of finance

Finance has been decentralized for a very long time until governments started putting controls on financial activities, mainly on the issuance of currency, money movement, creation and trading of financial securities (like stocks and bonds). Currently, almost all governments across the world force entities to use a central party for most of these activities. Central parties include central banks, clearinghouses (institutions that process the transfer of money or transactions), exchanges (institutions where securities, money, etc. are traded), registrars (institutions that record company details, etc.), and custodians (entities that hold securities, money and other assets on behalf of investors). Because of governmental regulations, in most countries, these activities are allowed to be done only by a limited number of entities and require licenses. This centralization of finance happened only in the last century or so. The reasons for the regulations are to increase efficiency or to improve trust amongst various market participants. Increasingly, technology is solving both of these problems, i.e. efficiency and trust. We are at a juncture where we can use solutions that allow market participants to efficiently

---

[2] Jefferson, T., Lipscomb, A. A. (ed.), and Bergh, A. E. (ed.) (1905). *The writings of Thomas Jefferson.* Washington, DC: Thomas Jefferson Memorial Association of the United States. Vol. 13-14, Page 421.

transact without a trusted third party. If the government removes the regulations on having only licensed operators to execute certain financial activities, the market will be able to design its own decentralized mechanisms to perform activities that are undertaken by central entities today.

The decentralization of finance starts with the denationalization of money. As discussed in the chapter on money, restricting the issuance of private money is a hurdle in free markets. Fortunately, in the last decade or so, cryptocurrencies have emerged as a decentralized alternative to fiat currencies. Although there is a lot of buzz around cryptocurrencies, specifically Bitcoin, the transactions using cryptocurrencies are still limited. As awareness builds and better technologies come up to make cryptocurrency transactions more efficient, the adoption could pick up further. This freedom to use a currency of choice could be the fuel for the next wave of economic growth if governments do not restrict it. Once the core of finance, i.e. money is decentralized, other parts of finance including investment and lending will also get decentralized. The investment industry is already seeing disruptive innovations like investments through decentralized tokens on a blockchain. The lending industry is also seeing innovations in the form of P2P (peer to peer) etc.; these innovations could remove the hegemony of centralized institutions.

Decentralization of information

The information ecosystem has been centralized for a long time because of the cost of dissemination of information. The invention of the printing press reduced the cost of the spread of information significantly. Even then, information was restricted to large libraries and private/government entities for a long time. The Internet has virtually eliminated the cost of information dissemination. Information is now instantaneously available to anyone with access to the Internet. The Internet has been set up as a decentralized network of computers, which can share information with each other. As the Internet grew in size and power, it became more centralized - Internet Service Provides acting as gateways to the Internet became regulated and large private entities built walled gardens within which information flow was bounded. Within these walled gardens, user data was being gathered and harvested to make money. These walled gardens, typically social networks, tended towards natural monopolies because of network effects. The network effect is a phenomenon where the value of a service increases if more people are part of the service. Because of network effects, a few platforms with the largest users tend to dominate the market. Driven by these factors the Internet today is tending towards a more centralized structure, where a small number of players become the key entities for access to information. This centralization allows governments to censor the information and also reduces the optimal utilization of information. Decentralization will have to be driven by the more open architecture of information, with more control over private data by the user. Things are moving very fast in this space, as long as the government does not interfere and control free information flow, the market will soon find solutions to make information access more decentralized.

Decentralization is becoming more prevalent in every ecosystem because of several recent technological enhancements. The main force of decentralization has been the Internet, but in the last ten years, cryptography and related technologies have taken the spotlight. The Internet allows for a free flow of information; cryptographic technologies add privacy and security layers to the Internet. As cryptocurrencies have proved, cryptographic technologies can be extended to perform tasks in a decentralized fashion, which required a trusted central party earlier. For example, now cryptographic technologies can be used to store land records in a decentralized fashion whereas earlier one has to depend on a government-appointed registrar of land deeds. Similarly, cryptographic technologies can be used for communication between peers without the intervention of a central party. Blockchain is a specific technology that uses cryptography to enable a tamper-proof, decentralized ledger. This ledger itself can be used for a variety of use cases including decentralization of governance and finance. Blockchain and other cryptographic technologies help in furthering the decentralization trend in the information ecosystems.

To sum up, decentralization empowers liberty. It is especially important in three key ecosystems- governance, finance, and information. As long as the government does not put specific restrictions or promote centralized solutions, business and technological innovations will automatically find decentralized solutions that can scale and deliver services more efficiently. Before the invention of such technologies, one had to rely on a central trusted party for various information storage and transmission-related services. The trusted party is usually either managed by the government or it is licensed and regulated by the government. As a result, there is heavy governmental interference in activities requiring a central trusted party. A decentralized solution can replace the central counterparty. This can increase transparency, reduce corruption, and improve efficiency. As technological evolution decentralizes business ecosystems, the government should be consciously decentralized. In a society where some sort of collective action is unavoidable, decentralized government best supports the liberty and prosperity of the individual.

Chapter 9

On the role of technology

It's not a faith in technology. What's important is that you have a faith in people, that they're basically good and smart, and if you give them tools, they'll do wonderful things with them.[1]

- Steve Jobs

The motivation for technological innovation is to make life easier for humans, either through easing the workload or providing newer ways of fulfilling their needs like entertainment Technology increases the wealth of the world through an increase in productivity. It also gives more liberty to men to do other things they would rather prefer doing by reducing their workload. As a result, technological innovation, liberty, and prosperity have been closely linked to each other in the last two centuries. Liberty has helped in accelerating the speed of scientific and technological innovation. Technology has helped increase the prosperity of people across the world. Now, technology is helping liberty to spread to the masses through the democratization of information.

All private-market driven technological innovations aim to increase the productivity of land and labor. Traditionally economists count three factors of production: land, labor, and capital. They argue that capital increases productivity of land and labor, hence it is a factor of production. The argument goes something like this: let us say a farmer buys a tractor and uses it for farming. The tractor increases the productivity of land and the farmer. As the tractor is bought by a capital investment of the farmer, capital is the cause of productivity increase. But if we observe carefully, the tractor is built using natural resources (metal, etc.) and labor. It just happened that someone else other than the farmer has built the tractor; and that is because of the division of labor. So, even if we count the tractor as a contributing factor for productivity increase, it is coming from land and labor only - it is not being created out of thin air from bundles of money. To put it shortly, capital is

---

[1] Goodell, J. (2011). "Steve Jobs in 1994: The Rolling Stone interview." RollingStone.com [Web]. Retrieved from: https://www.rollingstone.com/culture/culture-news/steve-jobs-in-1994-the-rolling-stone-interview-231132/.

nothing but accumulated land and labor. What has increased the productivity of land and labor is not the capital but the invention of the tractor, in other words, technological progress. At a macro level, technological progress is the main factor for sustained growth in prosperity over the long term. Even at a micro level, companies with access to better technology can keep their costs low and increase their profitability than companies that have more capital.

Technology leading to an increase in productivity is not a novel idea. Economists have argued that in a liberal society, technological innovation is the most important and maybe the only factor contributing to increase in productivity, once the society achieves an efficient allocation of resources and labor through the force of economic liberty. Also, economic liberty itself fosters technological innovation. In the chapter on economic liberty, we have argued that in the last two hundred years, prosperity has come about because of liberal economic policies. Those policies, in addition to having helped towards efficient allocation of natural resources and labor to productive activities, have also created an environment where technological innovation is incentivized. In the long term, technology is also a fruit of labor. In a free economy, companies can decide whether to spend resources and labor on operational activities or long term research activities, which can produce technological innovations. Similarly, individuals can decide, based on market feedback, to specialize in immediately productive activities or in research activities. This feedback can automatically occur if there is an active market for various goods and services including research activities. Free markets ensure that the allocation between operational activities and research activities is done in an efficient way. Private entities will allocate resources to technological research if there is a promise of productive output in the future from that research. Companies regularly keep updating their technology to deliver their goods and services more efficiently. Even in technological fields where large amounts of resources are needed, like for example space travel or developing global communication grids, private entities have shown tremendous enterprise.

Technology increases productivity through various avenues, including better utilization of natural resources, automation of manual processes, and enablement of smaller businesses. Of these, automation and enablement are two important aspects that we need to consider in more detail as they have a direct impact on the liberty and prosperity of people. I will also look at some of the negatives of "Big Tech" that can impinge upon liberty.

Automation

Automation helps in reducing manual effort and increasing productivity. For the same amount of labor, it helps to produce more. Automation is the biggest driver of growth in a business and also in an economy. The large-scale industrial revolution that we have seen in the 18th century and the 19th century is the first big wave of automation. The most important of the inventions that have come out in this era have an effect on our lives even to this date. Some examples include automated spinning machines, steam engines, and construction equipment. We have seen many waves of automation since then. The twentieth century saw automation through the use of electronics and computers. The current century is seeing automation through communication technologies and artificial intelligence (AI) technologies. These technologies are getting shaped purely by market forces rather than by any governmental interventions. The good thing governments did is to not interfere in the process of innovation. Liberty and technological innovation are intertwined. Liberal economic policies ensure that man's labor is used most effectively and that leads to technological development. Liberal policies in Europe in the 18th and 19th century, and in several other countries, later on, have been the reason for this significant surge in technological innovation. If there were laws implemented to discourage automation like minimum employment requirements for companies or if subsidies are given out to encourage more manual labor, technological progress would be hindered. A case in point is the textile industry in India. After India's independence in 1947, the government decided to promote the handloom industry and gave heavy subsidies. This has resulted in low technology adoption and created a very low growth environment. This policy was one of the key policy mistakes of the Indian government that Milton Friedman pointed out in his book[2] and show *Free to Choose*.

Even though technological progress creates great wealth, in the short run, it can cause some disruptions to economic activity. Spinning machines replace manual handlooms and handloom workers will have to develop new skills to be relevant. This can make people anxious about technological changes. But it is a myth that automation significantly reduces the need for human capital in the long run. In the current century, there is increased anxiety about artificial intelligence (AI) and automation through robotics having an impact on jobs. If history shows anything it is that this anxiety is unwarranted. The concerns about technology causing job losses - technological unemployment - are not new. David Ricardo says in his book - On the Principles of Political Economy and Taxation - in the year 1821 - "the discovery and use of machinery may be attended with a diminution of gross produce; and whenever that is the case, it

[2] Friedman, M. and Friedman, R. D. (1980). *Free to choose: a personal statement*. New York City: Harcourt Brace Jovanovich.

will be injurious to the laboring class, as some of their number will be thrown out of employment, and population will become redundant, compared with the funds which are to employ it."[3] There is no doubt that technology can create short-term disruptions but not more than any other business process changes. The long-term effects of technological innovations have been only positive as seen by the wealth creation in the last couple of centuries. Jean-Baptiste Say countered Ricardo's concern by arguing that no producer will use technology to reduce production. If anything they will try to produce more given the amount of natural resources and labor available to them. As a result, technological innovations always increase the supply of goods and services. This will have a positive impact on everyone including the labor as the demand will rise to match the additional supply. The surplus labor created by technological disruption will automatically be absorbed in the reproductive activities as the market adjusts itself. To quote Say - "As each of us can only purchase the productions of others with his own productions – as the value we can buy is equal to the value we can produce, the more men can produce, the more they will purchase."[4]

There is an anxiety in the past decade (the 2010s) that the new technologies collectively called artificial intelligence (AI) can replace humans in a variety of jobs. The current scare about AI replacing humans in jobs and hence creating long-term unemployed "class" is unfounded. AI is to information processes what the spinning machine was to the textiles industry. The same scare we see about AI today was abundant in the 18th and 19th centuries about textile technologies. In fact, in England in the late 18th century there arose an organization called The Luddites, who went to the extreme of vandalizing textile machinery to protest against automation. Their pain is understandable but the innovation was inevitable. Countries that have not adopted technological advancements would only make their countrymen poorer. Like spinning machines, AI expansion will also be inevitable. And like the spinning machine, AI can also help in reducing the cost of production and distribution of goods and services. If in the far future, AI reduces jobs to the level that a large portion of humanity does not need to work as all needs of all humans will be satisfied, that also is not a problem as in that case each human can have a citizen's dividend to live a happy life. The citizen's dividend will be

---

[3] Ricardo, D. and Gonner, E. C. K. (ed.) (1891). *Principles of Political Economy and Taxation*. United Kingdom: G. Bell and sons. Page 381.

[4] Say, J. B. and Richter, J. (trans.) (1821). *Letters to Mr. Malthus on Several Subjects of Political Economy, and Particularly on the Cause of the General Stagnation of Commerce*. United Kingdom: Sherwood, Neely, and Jones. Page 3.

coming from the taxes collected on natural resources, land, and corporations, as discussed in the chapter on taxation. I do not see that happening anytime soon as we are nowhere near a scenario where we are producing enough for fulfilling all the needs of humanity. In the future when that happens, humans may have much more time to spend on leisure activities and have more freedom to choose to lead the life they want.

Enabling power of technology

E. F. Schumacher, a British economist, wrote a book in 1973 – *Small is Beautiful: A Study of Economics as if People Mattered.* The book, which became very influential, has two main points to make[5]: 1. Natural resources must not be treated as being infinitely available and 2. Bigger is not always better. Schumacher argued that appropriate technologies that can use lesser natural resources and promote more decentralization need to be developed. As the title of the book suggests, Schumacher supports an economy where smaller businesses thrive and staunchly opposes the maxim – "bigger is better". Although I agree with the end objective of his - a world that operates in a decentralized fashion using resources judiciously, I do not subscribe to his recommendations that such economics be forced upon people. If technologies supporting smaller enterprises are desirable by entrepreneurs and individuals, then I believe that free markets, left to themselves, can automatically promote the development of such technologies. Schumacher says that people are happier working for themselves in a cottage industry than working in a factory for a large corporation. If that is the case, as I also believe it to be, then free market forces will automatically incentivize the development of technology that will enable this. If people prefer to make their products or offer services from their own home rather than to go to a factory or an office, then they will be willing to pay for technologies that enable this. This is an incentive for technologists to work on such innovations, which help in running small industries profitably. In fact, such developments are already happening in the past couple of decades. I call this the enabling power of technology.

The key pillar of this enablement is information technology - an amalgamation of computation and digital communication technologies. Information technology has helped in the decentralization of a wide range of economic activities. It has helped small-scale businesses to compete with large corporations by giving an avenue to distribute their products, by reducing the cost of production, and by reducing information asymmetry.

---

[5] Schumacher, E. F. (1973). *Small is beautiful: Economics as if people mattered.* New York City: Harper & Row.

Today, a single person business can also sell goods on the Internet and compete with large retail stores. Not only distribution but the production also has become easier. For example, with very small amounts of capital, one can make a movie, publish a book, or make a music video. In the twentieth century, these activities usually involved large teams and a large amount of capital. Directly or indirectly, information technology has impacted each and every economic sector.

The next big innovation, which is still in the nascent stages, is 3D printing. 3D printing is a technology that allows people to print objects at home or in a small workshop. 3D printing technology can revolutionize production and help even small workshops to compete with large factories of the world. The technology needs to develop further before it can make a significant dent in people's lives though. Once it develops further, 3D printing technology can be the second big pillar of the enabling power of technology. The decentralized society that E. F. Schumacher has envisaged is becoming a reality, not because of government intervention but because of market-driven technological innovations.

Another pillar of the enabling power of technology is decentralized/small scale energy generation. As of now, most sources of energy - coal, petrol, wind, hydro, nuclear - are all managed by larger entities. Solar energy can be generated at a smaller scale but it is not enough to cater to all our energy needs. Once energy generation is decentralized, it will further enable smaller entities to sustain and compete in global markets. Solar energy seems to be the most viable alternative in this space. As in the case of 3D printing, there is more research and development required in energy generation as well.

The only part of the production value chain that cannot be decentralized easily is the extraction of natural resources (other than agriculture). Of course, agriculture can be easily decentralized, but extraction of oil, minerals, metals and other raw material required for the production of goods still requires economies of scale and capital. I'm not in a position at the moment to predict if somewhere in the future there could be a technology using which even a small household can mine minerals out of their plot of land, but I don't see that happening in the near future. Nevertheless, mining and extraction of natural resources could be a small part of the overall decentralized economy. All value addition after the extraction can be executed by smaller entities in a decentralized fashion.

From a purely free-market-economics perspective, technology also enables establishing of property rights clearly. For example with today's information technology, any violation of copyrights can be monitored easily on the Internet. New ways of monitoring through technology can lead to defining property rights more accurately. For example, fishing rights in a river or an ocean can be monitored and implemented through technological innovations. This can lead to newer markets or extend the efficiencies of existing markets.

The last two hundred years have seen the development of technologies that helped the bigger entities as these technologies required economies of scale and large capital to work effectively. For example, one could have started spinning cotton at home using manual methods, but to make cheaper and higher quality textiles, one needs to invest in machinery that requires scale and capital. But that tide has already started to turn. We are seeing small businesses benefiting from technology more. Like Schumacher, I imagine a future where an economy consists of a large number of small businesses spread across the world, with each business being mainly driven by an entrepreneur and some apprentices. These businesses will be more of a lifestyle business (like a professional trade) rather than entities looking to extract rent[6]. And this will be achieved through market forces rather than through governmental controls.

Negatives of Big Tech

Other than job losses, technology is also sometimes blamed for creating monopolies and centralization. "Big Tech" is a collective term often used to denote large, dominant players in technology. "Big Oil" was a similar term used for large oil-producing companies in the late 19th century and early 20th century. "Big Pharma" is another term used to denote large pharmaceutical companies. The arguments against Big Tech are that it helps governments to control more and Big Tech companies misuse their monopoly. The crusade against Big Oil in the late 19th century by the "progressive movement" led to several antitrust laws. These laws ensure that the sanctity of competition is maintained and large companies do not take advantage of their position to enter into anti-competitive practices. The laws are called antitrust laws as most large corporations in the US were set up as a trust around that time. Laws promoting competition have been in existence in Europe for a long time, but most modern competition laws begin with the antitrust legislation in the US at the end of the 19th century and the beginning of the 20th century. The concern that people had about Big Oil is similar to the concern people have for Big Tech now.

Specifically, there could be concerns that technology companies, especially information technology companies, can misuse their monopoly by breaching

---

[6] Rent is a term used in economics used to denote payment made for using properties like land, patents, licenses, etc.

the privacy of customers, not respecting customers' rights, and charging very high prices for a lower quality product. On the point of breach of privacy, the tech companies themselves can use the private data of the customer, or they can pass it on to governmental agencies thus encroaching upon the liberty of citizens. Because of these concerns, some antitrust proponents have been arguing that Big Tech should be broken up into smaller companies so that competition is restored in the market. The concerns are valid, but breaking companies up is not the right solution. Competition laws do not prohibit companies from becoming monopolies. The prospect of becoming a monopoly is a big driver for entrepreneurship and even innovation. Companies should be allowed to become large through accumulated profits, but not through unfair practices like cartelization, predatory pricing, bundling, etc. Existing competition laws should be good enough to counter such unfair practices. These laws can be applied to technology companies just the way they have been applied to various monopolies over the past hundred-odd years. Any act by a technology company that is aimed to reduce the competition to the disadvantage of the customers should be considered an unfair trade practice. Some unfair trade practices that are illegal under several competition laws can be applied to technology companies as well, including cartelization, predatory pricing, tying, discriminator pricing, etc.

An unfair practice that is specifically applicable to technology companies is the abuse of customer data, as technology companies have access to large amounts of data related to customers. The right to engage in economic activity freely does not give companies the right to cause damage to the property of others or to appropriate property of others. Property should include anything that is produced by a customer or a third party. From this perspective, the data generated by customers is the property of the customer. Similarly, the intellectual property generated by customers and other parties, like for example user-generated content on social media or news reported by online newspapers, is also a property of the person creating the intellectual property. The rights of the property owner have to be respected. This logic creates a case for data protection laws. Any data or content created by a customer or any party should belong to the creator and a technology company cannot annex the property without the explicit consent of the creator. If the definition of property is interpreted to include data and content generated by a person, there is no need for separate data protection laws. Nevertheless, given the complex nature of technology companies and their services, some governments feel that it is better to have a set of guidelines that aim to protect the privacy and the rights of customers. This approach has been taken up by the European Union, when they came up with Global Data Protection Regulation, although unfortunately, it has become a mammoth regulation with close to 100 sections. Several other countries are also in the process of designing data protection laws. If globally, countries take an over-regulation approach it can only hinder innovation and create artificial barriers for entry. Private data of customers should be protected through existing laws and if required a simple set of new guidelines.

The fewer regulations there are, the better it is for innovation in technology. Existing customer protection and safety regulations should be enough to create a conducive environment for businesses to develop new technologies that create value through automation, enablement, and newer ways of satisfying customers (through entertainment, etc.) There is no need for any kind of government intervention either to promote or to regulate technological progress. As technology progresses, it can create wealth and reduce poverty to a large extent and it can also create more time for activities that humans truly love like entertainment, spending time with family, adventure, arts, scientific pursuit, etc., thus giving more meaning to the liberty and prosperity achieved.

Chapter 10

On dealing with external shocks

Collective decisions might be needed in some circumstances, especially, those that are caused by external factors like wars, pandemics, and natural disasters. In such scenarios, quick decision-making and a uniform response across the country are needed. Individual behavior and market forces may not move fast enough to counter the shock. Also, there might be a need for deploying more concerted action like in the case of fighting a war or fighting a pandemic. In such scenarios, it might be argued that a more interventionist approach will be helpful to protect people and to support the economy. I will examine this claim critically and identify what kind of approach is appropriate under the overarching liberal framework. The topic has become very relevant in 2020 as a result of a widespread pandemic due to the Covid-19 virus. The topic will also be relevant in the future whenever there is an external threat to the lives and livelihoods of citizens of any country. Similar pandemic may not reappear in the near future, but, wars, natural calamities, and other unforeseen shocks cannot be ruled out. Such external shocks with a worldwide impact have been very sporadic after the end of World War II, but they were quite prevalent before that. Having said that, specific countries have undergone shocks from time to time, including wars with neighbors, tsunamis, earthquakes, storms, pandemics, etc. Although the measures taken for each of these will be different, we could come up with a generic underlying framework that can help us guide in various such scenarios especially with regards to economic matters.

I will look at each of the aspects of liberal economics, most importantly the role of the government, in the light of external shock in this chapter. I do not want to get into the specific policy decisions by the governments with regards to the ongoing pandemic of Covid-19, as the impact of policy measures to handle the situation is still uncertain. And I will stick only to the economic aspects of the policy measures. I will leave specific measures to contain the impact of the shock to the experts. The chapter is split into two sections. The first section - Dealing with the shock - identifies measures that have to be taken to control the impact of the shock. The second section - Recovering from the shock - discusses measures that have to be taken to support the economy after the shock.

Dealing with the shock

The primary role of the state in the times of external shocks is to protect citizens. Even in the lack of external shock, protecting the life and property of citizens is the main role of a government. This role gains even more significance when there is a direct threat to the life and property of a large number of citizens. The government needs to take policy decisions based on expert opinion to minimize losses to life and property. As these policy decisions require expertise, the decision-making process need not be based on the wants of the general citizenry. Some of these policy decisions could curtail the liberties of citizens, but that is not contrary to the key principles of this book. I have maintained that, although liberty is very important for achieving prosperity, when human life is concerned it takes secondary priority. For this very reason, universal basic income (UBI) is a justifiable policy even though it does not strictly adhere to free-market principles. The same logic, when extended to the scenarios of pandemic or war or some sort of natural calamity, supports measures to protect citizenry even if such measures restrict some liberties (like the freedom to move or congregate) temporarily. Liberties that do not interfere with dealing with the threat need not be impinged upon. Like for example, in the case of a pandemic, freedom of movement can be curtailed but there is no reason for freedom of expression to be restricted. Also, any restrictions imposed should be removed as soon as the threat ceases to exist.

Having an external threat can create a deep impact on businesses and the economy. Some economic activities may not be able to freely operate. For example, when there is a war, people may not be able to go out in the open for agricultural activities. In the case of a pandemic, people may not go to offices and work. This can disrupt economic activity. It is the role of the government to provide an environment where economic activity can continue to a large extent. Economic activity should continue as it is crucial not just for the prosperity of people but it is important for maintaining lives as well. Lives need not be lost only to an external threat, losing livelihoods can cause loss of lives as well. There should not be arbitrary restrictions on economic activities unless they severely threaten lives. Even in cases where there is a possibility of a threat to life, the first course of action should be to let the economic activity continue after taking enough precautions.

During an external shock, the government will be mostly constrained on resources. In such a case, the government should focus on infrastructure that helps fight the shock. If there is a pandemic, resources should be diverted to health care. Funding for long-term infrastructure projects and long-term defense spending can be reduced. If there is a war, resources should be diverted to war efforts. This seems like an obvious recommendation, but it is very hard to implement as large governments tend to move slowly in the relocation of funds. Also, government departments, after being accustomed to certain levels of budgets, tend to be reluctant to trim down. But it is important to trim down on spending that is not required immediately, just like a family or a company does. This can ensure resources for fighting the threat without increasing deficits.

During war or pandemics, governments tend to give elaborate regulations on restricting activities for protecting citizens. Given the complex nature of business ecosystems, it will not be easy to predict precisely what activity can be stopped and what cannot be stopped. Businesses are interconnected with each other. Rather than providing lengthy regulations and trying to be specific, regulations should be minimal and generic. For example, when there is a pandemic it is better to restrict all businesses where distancing between employees or customers cannot be maintained, rather than providing a long list of what is allowed and what is not. In the case of a war, any business that exposes employees or customers to attacks should be restricted. Such generic guidelines/rules should be interpreted by local authorities to restrict specific economic activity. This can ensure a minimal impact on economic activity.

As far as possible, the government should use less coercive measures to implement the guidelines. Having strict measures with heavy penalties/ punishments can prove counterproductive as people might rebel, but more importantly, there might be a genuine need for minor transgressions in some cases. The government shouldn't use the heavy hand of the law to implement restrictions, instead, it should take a more empathetic approach. The government should make education and awareness as the primary method to implement restrictions. In situations where only a limited activity can be allowed (for example, air travel), the controlling should be done based on market-driven methods rather than randomly. For example, if the government wants to limit the number of flights, rather than arbitrarily deciding which airlines to be allowed to fly, it should auction the rights of flying. The cost of the license to fly can be passed on to the customers. This can achieve three things together: limit the number of flights, allow travel that is most valuable for the economy, and raise revenue for the government in a constrained economy.

Recovering from the shock or why stimulus is a bad policy

The real work on the economy starts after the shock gets over. After an external shock, most businessmen and economists want a governmental intervention. Even free-market supporters tend to argue for the government to provide a "stimulus" to the economy when there is a crisis. A stimulus is a government action intended to increase economic activity. A stimulus is usually provided as a fiscal stimulus or monetary stimulus. Fiscal stimulus is a policy action where the government spends more money either by directly giving money to individuals and companies or by investing money on infrastructure and other projects. The argument supporting fiscal stimulus is that total demand for goods and services in a country (called Aggregate Demand by economists) can fall during a shock and thus additional demand needs to be generated through government spending. Monetary stimulus is where a central bank lends money at cheap rates so that companies needing money can borrow at low interest rates.

There are several fallacies in the argument that government spending as part of fiscal stimulus, can revive the economy or that it is the best way to revive the economy. Firstly, in a free market, there is no strong reason for Aggregate Demand to fall below the quantity of goods and services produced in an economy (Aggregate Supply). When there is a shock, the incomes of people tend to drop as business revenues drop and employment opportunities also reduce. This causes a simultaneous drop in demand and supply. But, as supply increases, post the shock, demand will automatically pick up. If the demand is low, prices of goods will adjust to a level where demand will equal supply. As incomes of people pick up and people can afford more goods, the demand and prices will automatically go up. The free market ensures that demand always catches up with the supply. This idea has been first explored in the 19th century by the classical liberal economist, Jean-Baptiste Say, whose arguments can be summarized as: "supply creates its own demand"; this statement is known as Say's law, as it reflects the arguments presented in his book: *A treatise on political economy; or the production, distribution, and consumption of wealth*[1]. Say's law does not say that there will not be any excess supply of a particular product. That can happen, but a general glut of excessively produced products across the board cannot exist. For this reason, some economists, especially economists from Austrian School, consider using the terms Aggregate Demand (AD) and Aggregate Supply (AS) to describe economic processes unwarranted. In an economy, we can observe only the total quantity of goods produced, which will be equal to the total goods consumed. Thus government spending will only cause further trouble as it will keep the prices high and hence unaffordable for some citizens.

Secondly, even if the segregation of economic analysis into Aggregate Demand and Aggregate Supply is accepted, in the event of external shock, the most affected part of the economy is the supply side. When there is a shock,

---

[1] Say, J. B. and Prinsep, C. R. (trans.) (1855). *A treatise on political economy; or the production, distribution, and consumption of wealth*. Philadelphia: Lippincott, Grambo & Co.

factories shut, distribution networks breakdown, and production activities, in general, get hurt the most. Increasing the demand side using government spending does very little to revive this. If anything, increasing the demand without increasing production activity can cause inflation in the economy, which can further aggravate the situation.

Thirdly, to fund the stimulus, the government will have to tax citizens, if not immediately then at some point in the future. Hence, spending by the government will lead to a reduction in spending by individuals and companies. Even if the government gives back some part of the stimulus directly to individuals or companies, it is just a form of relocating wealth from one segment of the economy to another. To make it worse, as government spending is decided by a group of people rather than by the market, it may not be efficient. It is always better to leave the money in the hands of individuals and companies who take decisions based on their needs and market prices, thus contributing to the efficiency of the market.

Having rejected fiscal stimulus as a response to external shocks, let us examine the effectiveness of the monetary stimulus. Contrary to fiscal stimulus, monetary stimulus aims to increase the money supply. This is usually achieved by the central bank buying government bonds (also called quantitative easing). Quantitative Easing (QE) puts money in the hands of banks and others who own bonds. The hope is that this money will be used to give more loans to individuals and companies who will use it for producing and/or consuming more goods. The fallacy of the argument is that increasing money in the economy does not create wealth. Real wealth is created when goods available in the economy increase. Any increase in money supply benefits the entities that receive the money first and it will only relocate wealth. Of course, when the economy goes into recession, the interest rates in the economy have to go down to reflect this (as investments may not give enough returns). But this should happen through market forces and not through centralized manipulation. Nevertheless, in the current scenario, where short-term interest rates are not completely determined by the market, there is a case for the government or its agency, the central bank to reduce the interest rates if there is a shock to the economy. But anything beyond that, for example, central banks directly giving loans to some entities or buying corporate bonds and equities will create distortionary effects and moral hazards.

Does this mean that the government cannot or should not act in the face of an economic slowdown caused by an external shock? Mostly, in a completely free-market-driven economy, there is no need for any government intervention other than to protect life and property. The free market will enforce corrective moves to take the economy to the most optimal level. Having said that, in the current world, as most economies do not work in a completely liberalized economy, there are a few steps the governments could take to precipitate the recovery. These steps include tax reduction, interest rate reduction, deregulation, and increased safety nets.

The government can reduce taxes. Taxes create distortionary effects on the market. As I have argued in the chapter on taxation, most taxes should be thrown out of the window anyway. But in the current world, several taxes are levied on various economic activities. The government can let go of some taxes to provide relief to individuals and businesses. Specifically, consumption taxes like value-added tax or goods and services tax can be axed in the face of a slowdown because of external shock. Reducing consumption tax can have a uniform effect on all goods and services. It will help the poor more, as the amount of goods they consume is high as a percentage of their income.

The central bank can reduce interest rates. In a perfectly free economy, when there is shock, the interest rates on risk-free instruments like government bonds and interest on central bank deposits should drop significantly and may even go to zero or negative. That is because of the reduced opportunities in the market. This does not happen in the current world as short-term interest rates are controlled by the central bank usually. In such a case, the central bank should take steps to ensure the interest rates are low. This can include buying short-maturity government bonds (if they are used to manage money supply) and reducing the interest rates on central bank deposits. This logic should not be extended to buying corporate bonds or other risky assets by the central bank, as corporate bonds involve credit risk and their interest rates increase in a free market when there is a shock to the economy.

The government can remove some restrictions/regulations on businesses. Several regulations and restrictions stop the economy from rebounding quickly. Some examples include - wage restrictions, banking regulations, and regulation of rents. Minimum wage requirements are aimed to help people get enough income but these requirements can be counterproductive as employers may tend to reduce operations rather than paying the high wage requirement. This will be detrimental to both the employer and the employees. If wage restrictions are eliminated, employers can choose to employ people at the right market price. Similarly, banking regulations that restrict banks from renegotiating loans, can be detrimental to both the bank and the borrower. If banks are allowed to freely renegotiate loan terms then banks and borrowers together can come up with an optimal renegotiated contract. Several such regulations cause the market to not function efficiently. These regulations are not needed in a normal course. But they can make matters worse in the face of external shocks. Liberalization of such regulations can help the economy recover fast.

The government should not put price controls. Usually, governments tend to put controls on the prices of certain goods to make them accessible to everyone. Well-intentioned that might be, it can dampen the recovery process. Market prices act as an incentive mechanism and feedback for producers. If they are capped artificially, the producers will not have the incentive to produce more. The market will not know what the true value of a good is. This can hurt the already bruised economy further.

The government should provide a safety net for the poor. The sole purpose of universal basic income is to support individuals in the time of turbulence. UBI becomes all the more relevant when there is an external shock. If countries do not have a UBI or if the UBI is not comprehensive enough to provide safety to all the vulnerable, the government should introduce UBI or some such direct support to most vulnerable individuals. The UBI scheme should be wide enough to cover all unemployed poor so that they can tide over the crisis. Continued high UBI can create a moral hazard where people do not go back to work. Hence the UBI should be enough to act as a safety net but it should not be high enough to satisfy all the needs.

The government should not bail out companies. The arguments supporting UBI should not be extended to companies. Bailing out companies, especially large companies, can lead inefficiencies to accumulate in the economy. Companies that have not operated with prudence should be let go into bankruptcy. Any bailout will benefit the shareholders who have been reckless the most. If a company goes bankrupt, two things happen: its current shareholders are wiped out and the debtors or whoever can pay off the debtors will take over its assets and operations. The new company or other competitors will typically absorb the employees. What about small and medium companies? They too need not be bailed out as long as individuals losing income opportunities are protected through direct benefits. Any corporate bailout, in addition to fostering irresponsible behavior, is also very expensive and paid by other taxpayers.

Governments should not fund increased deficits through printing money. Some of the above measures can increase the deficit of the government. There are three ways to fund this gap: 1. Increase taxes, 2. Borrow using bonds, 3. Print money. The government should ideally take the second option. The first option of increasing taxes will further slow down the economy. The third option of printing money can lead to hyperinflation, as discussed in the chapter on money. Governments in the past have issued war bonds to fund wars. Citizens tend to invest in war bonds or maybe even pandemic bonds even if they get a lower interest rate than the market out of patriotism. Such bonds can fund the efforts during the shock and after the shock. Those bonds can be paid back using future taxes with some austerity incorporated into government spending.

No doubt, external shocks can create a dent in the economy. In the face of adversity, families, and companies tend to spend on what is important, reduce unnecessary expenses, and behave more prudently. The same applies to countries as well. Countries need to reduce unnecessary expenditures and focus on what is most important, i.e. protecting the weak and the poor. During both the World Wars, countries involved undertook severe austerity measures to conserve goods, people sacrificed comforts, and companies did not expect large-scale bailouts from the government. After the wars, the economy corrected quickly to generate enough employment and growth for everyone. This gives us confidence that once the external shock goes away, market forces can help the economy recover very fast. All the liberal principles that we have discussed elsewhere in the book are applicable even in the post-shock situation. There is no need for a drastically different economic framework for dealing with the after-effects of shocks.

Chapter 11

On the path to prosperity

Through millennia, ever since humans became self-aware, every human's biggest pursuit has been to make life better for herself, i.e. become more prosperous. This pursuit of prosperity is what drives economic activity, technological progress, and even the development of society. Closely intertwined with the pursuit of prosperity is the desire for liberty. Liberty and prosperity are linked to each other in more than one way. The value of prosperity is limited if there is no liberty to use prosperity as a person deems fit. Similarly, just having liberty is meaningless if a person does not have the ways and means for leading a happy life. Apart from this two-way relationship, it is a happy coincidence that having liberty especially on the economic front can automatically lead to the prosperity of a large set of population.

Liberal economic policies coupled with the rule of law and technological progress of the last two centuries have lifted several millions of people out of poverty. This scale of wealth generation has not been seen in any period before this, in the history of the world. At the same time, the number of poor has also increased tremendously, in absolute terms if not in proportion to the population. This dichotomy can be explained by a difference in policy implementations across countries. Specifically, lack of liberty in economic fronts and lack of protection of rights has put citizens of some countries at a disadvantage compared to those of other countries. Even at this point, turning the tide of increasing poverty is not tough. Systematic application of the principles of liberty can help the billions who are living in poverty and even those who are not achieving the full prosperity that they deserve. The time taken to turn the tide is not very high as has been seen in countries that liberalized their economic policies in the latter half of the 20th century and became quite prosperous by the start of this century. I sincerely hope that more countries turn towards economic liberalism to solve their poverty and other problems. Even countries that have high per capita income can aim to achieve more equitable prosperity through further liberalization.

Every country is at a different stage of liberalization and economic development. Every country may not implement all the recommendations of this book immediately. But the path towards liberalization has to start for every country to end the cycle of poverty. I will relook at the necessary ingredients of a liberal society that can facilitate universal prosperity. All of these ingredients are important, maybe with different levels of priority. If implemented, I believe, these recommendations can see another wave of prosperity much stronger than what we have seen in the last couple of centuries. That can put a period to poverty once and for all. The rest of the chapter summarizes the recommendations spread throughout the book.

Rights protecting, minimal, decentralized government

The most important role of government, in a fully liberal society, is to protect the citizens and their rights equitably. This role may also be framed as the rule of the law. Rights of citizens form the basis of liberty and the rule of law, which ensures those rights are protected, is a precursor to liberty and prosperity. Rule of law establishes justice, creates an equitable society, and provides a predictable environment. All of these are important factors for a free society and a free market to work efficiently. The right to life is the most important right. Several other rights need to be protected by the law enforcement division of the government. From the perspective of economics, the most important rights are the right to own property and the right to pursue a profession/business of choice. The rights of citizens have to be protected from external aggressors, and internal aggressors. Thus, national defense, law and order become key functions of a government.

Apart from rights protection, the government's role should be minimal. If there is a need for regulating an industry or an economic activity, because of high impact on life and property of customers, employees, or other stakeholders, the regulation should be minimal and only address the specific risk involved. Generic customer protection laws should be sufficient to protect customers in a wide range of industries and there is no need for stringent regulations for each industry. Other than regulation, governments usually get involved in infrastructure development and welfare programs. For these activities as well, the role of government should be minimized. The infrastructure development role of the government should be restricted to areas where private entities cannot take the role because they may not be able to obtain the right of way easily. As regards to welfare, direct transfer of money through guaranteed income should be preferred where ever possible than providing goods, services, and subsidies. Lastly, the government should especially not run any businesses. On the whole, the smaller the government, the better it is because the private market will be able to allocate resources more efficiently. A small government also means that individuals are taxed less to fund it. This is a big incentive for individuals to produce more.

Whatever minimal role the government has should be executed in a decentralized fashion. Power should be spread out to various states and further to cities/municipalities as they are closer to the citizens and have better local information to make optimal decisions. The central government should retain a very small role, mainly consisting of defending the country and developing national regulations and infrastructure that affect the whole country. Local government bodies should collect local taxes and develop local infrastructure. Local bodies should be able to compete with each other in attracting economic activity. Sufficient freedom should be given to the local bodies to manage their policies.

A simplified, low tax regime

Most taxes disincentivize production and distort the market. Income taxes and consumption taxes are especially detrimental to the freedom of profession. An alternative to revenue collection through taxing income is to tax landholding. The idea is that land belongs to society and any holder of land should compensate society for the same. Tax on landholding can generate enough revenues to replace all other taxes if the government spending is curtailed severely. This is called a single tax regime. This has multiple benefits. Eliminating income tax incentivizes more production. It reduces land hoarding and encourages more efficient use of the scarce resource of land. It simplifies the tax system as there will not be any need for elaborate tax laws and individuals need not pay taxes or file tax returns. Although in reality, a single tax regime may not be completely viable, a reduction in income tax and an imposition of land tax is a good step in this direction. In the language of economics, land includes natural resources. Related to natural resource usage, a special tax on the extraction of natural resources should be charged to ensure they are not wasted. This tax is known as severance tax and can be applicable for oil extraction and mining of coal, metals, and minerals. Similar to severance tax is the Pigouvian tax, which is levied when an entity pollutes the environment. Pigouvian tax can be directly applied to the usage of petrol and other carbon-based energy resources. The justification of severance and Pigouvian taxes is that natural resources and the environment belong to society and any harm done by the economic activity should be compensated.

I have argued that income taxes should be eliminated. The argument was for income tax levied on individuals. As corporations are special entities that are formed because of the legal structure of a country, there is a justification for taxation on the income of corporate entities. In a way, corporate tax is a fee by corporations for using the jurisdiction of the country. Nevertheless, this corporate income tax, if levied, should be kept low. Apart from these taxes, ideally, there should not be any other levy or tax by the government. Specifically, consumption taxes like value-added tax and income tax on individuals should be eliminated. Irrespective of types of taxes levied, the overall taxation should be low and the taxation regime should be simple and easy to administer.

Limited role of central banks

Central banks have become the go-to institution for fighting recessions since the 1970s. But, several boom-bust cycles have shown that monetary policy (policies managing the economy through changing money supply by the central banks) only postpones the crisis and it is not truly effective. Leaving the management of the most important market in an economy - the money market - to a select few is inconsistent with free market-driven economic policy. Currently, central banks carry too much power and they need to be restricted. Monetary policy in an economy should be reduced to a simple rule that can be implemented algorithmically. This can bring in transparency and remove the power of a select few on the markets.

Apart from managing short term rates, central banks have taken up more innovative techniques like lending directly to banks (on top of standard liquidity facility) and buying long-term assets. These tools go way beyond money supply management. Such measures can lead to, in fact, in the past, they have led to, moral hazards where banks and other institutions take reckless risks with the assumption that the central bank will protect them. Such measures also increase income disparity as they increase the wealth of asset holders disproportionately more. Investors who take excessive leverage and invest in long-term, risky assets benefit from such policies. Any activity that involves risk, even if the risk is minuscule, should be left to the markets and not indulged in by central banks.

Central banks, sometimes, take up the additional role of regulating banks as they implement their monetary policy through the banking system. In some countries, central banks tend to overregulate banks and as a result, stifle growth severely. There is no need for elaborate banking regulation. If the central bank is only worried about the risk of a bank going bankrupt, central banks can use a risk-based supervision framework, where they ensure that banks have enough capital to cover all the risks they carry, rather than regulating every aspect of banking.

Denationalized Money

The monetary system most countries currently use involves fiat money. In this system, money has value because the government says it does. To protect the fiat money, countries do not allow other forms of money in the economy. This is in effect monopolization of money. As long as the government retains a monopoly on money, there is no incentive for it to have control over spending because in the worst case, it can always print more money. As we already know, printing money does not create wealth. Production of goods and services does. It is ideal for the governments to let go of their monopoly on money. When businesses and individuals are mostly free to create and sell several types of products, there is no reason why the same freedom should not be allowed for money as well. There is no need for restricting money to a single currency. The government should allow citizens to use any form of money that is convenient to them, be it currencies of other countries, privately issued money, or decentralized money (cryptocurrencies). Each currency can have its own monetary policy i.e. policy to determine how the price and supply of the currency are controlled. That will bring competition in money.

No bailing out of businesses

Governments, in the past, have bailed out several businesses, including banks. The logic they give is that the businesses being bailed out are too big to fail - either their failure causes a systemic impact or wide-scale job losses. Both of these arguments are not consistent with free-market economics. There is no need for a solution for business failures even in a recession or external shock, as business failure is in itself a solution to accumulated inefficiencies.

The logic given for bailouts is that some businesses, for example, banks will have several different customers across different industries so if a bank fails, the failure can have contagion effects. In a perfectly open and free market, competition ensures that there is no single entity whose failure can cause a widespread systemic risk. Each industry will have several competing players and risks in the economy are usually diversified across businesses. When a bank goes bankrupt, smaller customers are usually protected through a deposit insurance scheme. Larger customers can recover part of their losses when the assets of the bank are liquidated. In the long term, customers will make a provision for bankruptcies when dealing with banks and other entities in the market.

The second justification for bailing out of companies is that large companies employ several people and a large company going bankrupt will lead to job losses. In reality though, when a company goes bankrupt, usually its operations are taken over by the debt holders or another company. The operations are likely to continue, so the job losses will not be very drastic. Even in the case where operations are not restored, the services offered by a large company will be provided by several other competitors and new companies. These companies create new jobs, which will compensate for the job losses.

Bailing out of businesses is distortionary on many fronts. Firstly, bailing out of a failed business is unjust to companies that have managed risk well and have behaved prudently. Secondly, bailing out allows inefficient companies to remain in the economy thus impacting economic growth. Thirdly, bailing out creates a moral hazard where companies tend to take excessive risks.

Safety net through UBI

The economy is a dynamic entity. There is always change and turbulence. The turbulence is higher when there is an external shock or when there is a technological change. To protect citizens in the face of such changes, the government should provide universal basic income (UBI). UBI is a safety net that protects the poor who did not receive the benefit of liberal economics yet. In the liberal economic framework, UBI is justified on four fronts. Firstly, it could be a direct and sure-shot way to end poverty and protect millions of people dying from poverty. Secondly, UBI is a much better alternative to more distortionary welfare schemes like providing food, education, etc. Thirdly, UBI can provide support to people while they become employable by developing new skills. This can add to the productivity of the economy. Lastly, UBI is a correction of past injustices as poverty has accumulated over generations of exploitation.

Implementation of UBI has several challenges like abuse of the income, a disincentive to work, complexity in calculating the right amount of UBI, complexities in deciding eligibility criteria (if it is not universal), increase in deficits of the government, etc. Nevertheless, if all other interventionist programs of the government are reduced, government machinery can come up with efficient mechanisms to overcome these challenges. Universal basic income, coupled with non-interventionist government and free markets, can provide an opportunity to billions of poor to come out of poverty.

Glide-path for developed economies

At this stage, I want to go back to the question I asked at the beginning of the book - after several centuries of scientific management of economies, why are we still not at a stage where we can say there is universal prosperity? Definitely, it is not because of a lack of intention or hard work from economists and policymakers. We are lacking in achieving universal prosperity, mostly because of all the well-meaning interventions, which throttle liberty. Most interventions might start with a noble intention to protect someone. But in the process, governments take up more and more roles, eventually leading to extremely inefficient use of resources. Vested interests ensure that once a government takes on power, it is not let go of. Thus, even incremental steps of intervention will eventually lead to a bloated government. Putting people back in control of their economic freedom can reverse this trend. As discussed above and elaborated throughout the book, the path to this is through four simple paradigms: rule of law, free markets, limited government, and universal basic income.

The glide-path towards universal prosperity and liberty is different for different countries based on their current status. More developed countries usually have already implemented some liberal economic policies. Even then, most countries lack full liberty. Developed countries can build on the rule of law that they have established over several centuries. Although some rich countries have moved away from a completely free market in the last fifty years, they have a solid base of rights protecting governments, which can make it easy to roll back some of the interventionist policies. The big interventions from the government come in four forms in the more developed countries: welfare schemes, regulations, intervention in money supply, and corporate bailouts. For giving more liberty to individuals all of these forms of intervention should be scaled down.

First and foremost, several welfare schemes like free or subsidized housing, free education, etc. should be replaced by a universal basic income. This can reduce the expenses of the government without reducing the benefits to individuals. As UBI will require much less overhead, a big portion of the money spent by the government will reach the citizens. The citizens can spend this money as per their needs. As this reduces the expenses of the government, it can reduce taxes on income (individual and corporate both). Eventually, the government can eliminate most taxes and keep only tax on land. Next, the governments of developed economies need to scale down regulations. Most of the industries in the developed world are free to operate, except for financial services and healthcare/pharmacy. Both of these industries are regulated to protect the customers. Regulations in these industries stifle innovation and impact growth. For protecting customers, generic customer protection laws should be sufficient. The competition will ensure the emergence of private certification bodies that will be able to bridge the information gap that customers and companies might have. The elephant in the room, when it comes to large developed economies is monetary policy. Absolute control of money supply and manipulation of the money market by a select few introduces much inefficiency. Specifically, it allows inefficient banks and companies to continue working and it causes a large wealth gap. This has to end. The role of central banks should be trimmed and money should be denationalized. More forms of money should be allowed to evolve. Finally, all forms of corporate bailouts should stop. Any corporate bailout comes from taxpayers' money. Bailouts affect the middle-class taxpayers, who typically do not own large amounts of shares in companies, negatively. Thus, further increasing the wealth gap.

In a developed economy, all of these steps can typically be implemented in a timeframe of five years. The government can scale down expenditure and taxes in tandem. Once implemented, the biggest beneficiaries of this further liberalization will be the poorer section. Even if the growth of overall GDP does not improve significantly, these steps will create universal prosperity because the wealth of the poorer lot can increase.

Glide-path for middle and low-income economies

The priorities for lower-income countries will be different than those of developed countries. The key steps towards liberalization in lower-income countries will be - establishing rule of law, reducing government expenditures, and removing regulations on trade and businesses. Establishing the rights of citizens and enforcing them is the first and the most important step towards prosperity. The right to life, property, and profession are the principal rights from the perspective of economics. But other rights, like freedom of expression, are also important from the perspective of liberty. Citizens should be protected not only from other aggressors but also from the government itself sometimes. A safe environment where citizens can lead the life in the way they want to and carry out the profession of their choice will go a long way in improving their wealth. Even before the liberal economic policies were fully implemented in the UK, the UK had a long history of the rule of law, starting in the thirteenth-century charter Magna Carta. The rule of law established in the UK through centuries formed the basis of the rule of law in the US after its independence. This fostered the environment required for the development of various liberties. For universal prosperity, the rule of law has to be replicated around the world. Less developed economies have to consciously improve on this factor.

Secondly, governments of developing economies should tightly control their expenditures as unlike in the case of developed economies, the market may not forgive high expenditures. Any lax in fiscal prudence can lead to a debt or currency crisis. It is not necessary to have a large government to run a country. A decentralized government structure with a small central government is enough. Industry-specific departments in the government should be abolished. The central government can simply consist of limited functions like finance, defense, and external affairs. Most other functions can be delegated to states and local governments. Governments should completely get away from the business. All government-owned enterprises should be privatized.

Licensing requirements and restriction of trade and businesses should be eliminated. International and domestic trade should be allowed to happen freely. Within the country, trade across the borders of the state should not be restricted and trade with businesses outside the country should be free of controls and tariffs. Any tariffs on imports might seem like a measure to protect domestic businesses, but they are impediments to progress as domestic businesses will not improve efficiencies when protected. Also, tariffs are eventually passed on to the consumers, so middle and low-income consumers get affected by the tariffs the most.

As low-income countries still do not have high public spending on healthcare and education, the right path for welfare for them would be to provide direct benefit through universal basic income. Initially, UBI need not be universal, as the government may not be able to afford it. UBI can be started at a low scale to help the poorest of the poor and then slowly scaled up.

The path for achieving liberty and prosperity for a low or middle-income country will be much tougher than a higher income country. Governments should first work on getting the basics (like rights protection) right and then work towards reducing the size of the government at the same time rationalizing taxes. The time frame for establishing liberty in a low and middle-income country will be more than ten years. But the effects of some of the liberalization measures can lead to immediate fruits. Nevertheless, this requires a national consensus and a long-term, stable vision from the government. Voter awareness, education of policymakers is key for this.

Arbitrary governance without any concern for the rule of the law, heavy governments with bloated overheads, unnecessary regulations, lack of freedom to engage in economic activity of choice, and inefficient implementation of welfare programs are the hindrances for universal prosperity. It is time to pare all of these hindrances off with a single razor: liberty. Liberty and freedom have been the bedrock of modern society. Several millions of people have laid down their lives, and continue to do so even today, to ensure we live in a society free from despots, fascists, inequality, and unjust laws. It is our duty that their sacrifice is put to good use and the liberty that they seek is available to everyone. The fact that several billions of people are living in poverty is an affront to the sacrifices made to achieve liberty and freedom. Full liberty leading to universal prosperity should be the ultimate goal of humans. With a bit of effort from politicians, economists, think tanks, and various policy-making bodies, there is no reason why we cannot achieve universal liberty and prosperity across the world in the next half a century.

Bibliography

Further Reading

Friedman, M. and Friedman, R. D. (1980). *Free to choose: A personal statement.* New York City: Harcourt Brace Jovanovich.

George, H. (1973). *Progress and poverty; an inquiry into the cause of industrial depressions and of increase of want with increase of wealth: The remedy.* New York City: AMS Press.

Hayek, F. A. (1960). *The constitution of liberty.* Chicago: University of Chicago Press.

Hayek, F. A. (1974). "The pretence of knowledge - Prize lecture." NobelPrize.org [Web]. Retrieved from: https://www.nobelprize.org/prizes/economic-scien ces/1974/hayek/lecture/.

Hayek, F. A. (1990). *Denationalisation of money - The argument refined.* London: Institute of Economic Affairs.

Data Sources

Bank of England (2020). *A millennium of macroeconomic data.* BankofEn gland.co.uk [Web]. Retrieved from: https://www.bankofengland.co.uk/- /media/boe/files/statistics/research-datasets/a-millennium-of- macroeconomic-data-for-the-uk.xlsx.

Federal Reserve Bank of St. Louis (2020). *Effective federal funds rate.* StLouisFed.org [Web]. Retrieved from: https://fred.stlouisfed.org/series/ FEDFUNDS.

Federal Reserve Bank of St. Louis (2020). *Velocity of M2 money stock.* StLouisFed.org [Web]. Retrieved from: https://fred.stlouisfed.org/series/M2V.

Federal Reserve Bank of St. Louis (2020). *M1 money stock.* StLouisFed.org [Web]. Retrieved from: https://fred.stlouisfed.org/series/M1.

Federal Reserve Bank of St. Louis (2020). *M2 money stock.* StLouisFed.org [Web]. Retrieved from: https://fred.stlouisfed.org/series/M2.

International Monetary Fund (2020). *Inflation rate, average consumer prices - Annual percentage change.* IMF.org [Web]. Retrieved from: https://www.imf. org/external/datamapper/PCPIPCH@WEO/VEN.

Ortiz-Ospina, E. (2016). *Taxation.* OurWorldinData.org [Web]. Retrieved from: https://ourworldindata.org/taxation.

Our World in Data (2017). *Central government expenditure as share of GDP.* OurWorldinData.org [Web]. Retrieved from: https://ourworldindata.org/gra pher/total-gov-expenditure-gdp-wdi.

The Heritage Foundation (2020). *Index of economic freedom.* Heritage.org [Web]. Retrieved from: https://www.heritage.org/index/excel/2020/index20 20_data.xls.

The World Bank (2020). *GDP per capita (current US$).* WorldBank.org [Web]. Retrieved from: https://data.worldbank.org/indicator/NY.GDP.PCAP.CD.

The World Bank (2020). *Income share held by lowest 10%.* WorldBank.org [Web]. Retrieved from: https://data.worldbank.org/indicator/SI.DST.FRST.10.

Other References

Arrow, K. and Debreu, G. (1954). "Existence of an equilibrium for a competitive economy." Econometrica. Vol. 22.

Elwell, C. K. (2011). "Brief history of the gold standard in the United States." Fas.org (Congressional Research Service) [Web]. Retrieved from: https://fas.org/sgp/crs/misc/R41887.pdf.

Friedman, M. (1960). *A program for monetary stability.* New York City: Fordham University Press.

Friedman, M. (1994). *Money Mischief: Episodes in Monetary History.* United States: Houghton Mifflin Harcourt.

Friedman, M. and Schwartz, A. J. (1963). *A monetary history of the United States, 1867-1960.* Princeton: Princeton University Press.

Goodell, J. (2011). "Steve Jobs in 1994: The Rolling Stone interview." RollingStone.com [Web]. Retrieved from: https://www.rollingstone.com/culture/culture-news/steve-jobs-in-1994-the-rolling-stone-interview-231132/.

Hayek, F. A. (1978). *Law, legislation and liberty.* Chicago: University of Chicago Press Economics Books.

Hayek, F. A. (1994). *The road to serfdom. 50th anniversary edition with a new introduction by Milton Friedman.* Chicago: University of Chicago Press.

House of Commons Debate 12 February 1907 vol 169 cc58-152. Retrieved from: https://api.parliament.uk/historic-hansard/commons/1907/feb/12/kings-speech-motion-for-an-address.

Jefferson, T., Lipscomb, A. A. (ed.), and Bergh, A. E. (ed.) (1905). *The writings of Thomas Jefferson.* Washington, DC: Thomas Jefferson Memorial Association of the United States.

Keynes, J. M. (1936). *The general theory of employment, interest and money.* New York City: Harcourt, Brace.

King, M. L. (1967). *Where do we go from here: Chaos or community?.* New York City: Harper & Row.

Kresge, S. and Wenar, L. (eds.) (1994). *Hayek on Hayek: An autobiographical dialogue.* London: Routledge.

Locke, J. (2004). *Second Treatise of Government.* United States: Barnes & Noble Books.

Menger, C., Dingwall, J. (trans.), and Hoselitz, B. F. (trans.) (1994). *Principles of economics.* Grove City, PA: Libertarian Press.

Olson, R. (2014). "Using the index of economic freedom: A practical guide." Heritage.org [Web]. Retrieved from: https://www.heritage.org/international-economies/report/using-the-index-economic-freedom-practical-guide.

Paine, T. and Foner, P. S. (ed.) (1945). *The Complete Writings of Thomas Paine.* United States: Citadel Press.

Ricardo, D. and Gonner, E. C. K. (ed.) (1891). *Principles of Political Economy and Taxation.* United Kingdom: G. Bell and sons.

Say, J. B. and Prinsep, C. R. (trans.) (1855). *A treatise on political economy; or the production, distribution, and consumption of wealth.* Philadelphia: Lippincott, Grambo & Co.

Say, J. B. and Richter, J. (trans.) (1821). *Letters to Mr. Malthus on Several Subjects of Political Economy, and Particularly on the Cause of the General Stagnation of Commerce.* United Kingdom: Sherwood, Neely, and Jones.

Schumacher, E. F. (1973). *Small is beautiful: Economics as if people mattered.* New York City: Harper & Row.

Smith, A. (2002). *The wealth of nations.* Oxford, England: Bibliomania.com Ltd. Loc.gov (Library of Congress) [Web]. Retrieved from: https://lccn.loc.gov/2002564559.

Taylor, J. B. (1993). "Discretion versus policy rules in practice." Carnegie-Rochester Conference Series on Public Policy, Elsevier. Vol. 39(1).

The World Bank (2018). "Nearly half the world lives on less than $5.50 a day." WorldBank.org [Web]. Retrieved from: https://www.worldbank.org/en/news/press-release/2018/10/17/nearly-half-the-world-lives-on-less-than-550-a-day.

Thoreau, H. D. (2016). *Civil Disobedience.* United States: Xist Publishing.

Walras, L. (2013). *Elements of pure economics.* United Kingdom: Taylor & Francis.

Zwolinski, M. (2013). "The libertarian case for a basic income." Libertarianism.org [Web]. Retrieved from: https://www.libertarianism.org/columns/libertarian-case-basic-income

Index

CPSIA information can be obtained
at www.ICGtesting.com
Printed in the USA
LVHW080321150421
684566LV00019B/133/J

9 781648 891984